# SOCRATES ON TRIAL

More than 2,400 years after his death, Socrates remains an iconic but controversial figure. To his followers, he personified progressive Greek ideals of justice and wisdom. To his detractors, he was a corruptor of the young during wartime and one of the reasons Athens suffered its humiliating defeat at the hands of Sparta in 404 BC. Socrates' story is thus one of historic proportions and his unyielding pursuit of truth remains controversial and relevant to the present day.

*Socrates on Trial* presents the story of Socrates as told to us by Aristophanes, Plato, Xenophon, and others. The play uses fresh language to emphasize what is important in the works of these ancient authors, while at the same time remaining faithful to the general tenor and tone of their writings. Andrew Irvine has created a script that not only fits comfortably into the space of a single theatrical performance, but is also informative and entertaining. Suited for informal dramatic readings as well as regular theatrical performances, *Socrates on Trial* will undoubtedly appeal to instructors and students alike.

Complete with production and classroom notes, this modern recasting of the Socrates story will make riveting reading both inside and outside the classroom.

ANDREW D. IRVINE is a professor in the Department of Philosophy at the University of British Columbia.

ANDREW D. IRVINE

# Socrates on Trial

A Play Based on Aristophanes' *Clouds*
and Plato's *Apology, Crito,* and *Phaedo*
Adapted for Modern Performance

UNIVERSITY OF TORONTO PRESS
Toronto Buffalo London

© University of Toronto Press 2008
Toronto Buffalo London
Printed in the U.S.A.

Reprint 2010, 2014

ISBN 978–0-8020–9783–5 (cloth)
ISBN 978–0-8020–9538–1 (paper)

Printed on acid-free paper

---

**Library and Archives Canada Cataloguing in Publication**

Irvine, A.D.
Socrates on trial : a play based on Aristophanes' Clouds and Plato's Apology,
Crito, and Phaedo, adapted for modern performance / Andrew D. Irvine.

Includes bibliographical references.
ISBN 978–0-8020–9783–5 (bound)
ISBN 978–0-8020–9538–1 (pbk.)

1. Socrates – Drama.   2. Aristophanes. Clouds.   3. Plato. Apology.   4. Plato. Crito.
5. Plato. Phaedo.   I. Plato   II. Aristophanes   III. Title

PS8617.R84S63 2007      C812'.6      C2007-905351-3

---

University of Toronto Press acknowledges the financial assistance to its publishing
program of the Canada Council for the Arts and the Ontario Arts Council.

University of Toronto Press acknowledges the financial support for its publishing
activities of the Government of Canada through the Book Publishing Industry
Development Program (BPIDP).

# Contents

# Acknowledgments

This retelling of the story of Socrates is based on a variety of ancient sources, but especially on Aristophanes' *Clouds* and Plato's *Apology*, *Crito*, and *Phaedo*. The storylines from all four works have been abridged. In the case of the *Crito* and the *Phaedo*, all of Plato's original language has been reworked. In the case of the *Clouds* and the *Apology*, most of the original language has been reworked, although some wording has been incorporated from two separate English-language translations: Ian Johnston's translation of the *Clouds* (Malaspina University-College, 2004) and Steve Wexler's translation of the *Apology* (University of British Columbia, 2006). I am grateful to both translators for generously granting me permission to adapt their memorable translations in this way. Readers wanting to enjoy the longer, original translations are encouraged to do so by contacting the translators directly.

I also want to thank David Armstrong of Sydney University for giving me the initial idea of performing these works; Joan Bryans of Vital Spark Theatre Company for her expert guidance in contemporary performance requirements and for suggesting the title *Socrates on Trial*; David Gallop and Mark McPherran for their invaluable advice on the project as a whole; Paul Bartha, Sylvia Berryman, Ian Brooks, John Camp, Julie Cohen, Danny Daniels, Miranda Duffy, John Harris, Rachel Hertz, Hugh Hunter, Joan Irvine, Don Morrison, Ira Nadel, Tony Podlecki, Roger Seamon, Sandy Slater, Steve Wexler, John Woods, and three anonymous referees for their many helpful suggestions; David Gallop, Doug Hutchinson, and Steve Wexler for their patient guidance in the correct pronunciation of Greek names; The Law Foundation of British Columbia, Branch MacMaster Barristers & Solicitors, Singleton Urquhart LLP, Sutherland and Associates, Whitelaw Twining Law Corporation, and the Vancouver Bar Association's *The Advocate*, together with the Faculty of Law, the Department of Philosophy, and the Department of Theatre, Film, and Creative Writing at the University of British Columbia for generously sponsoring the play's premiere performance; and Len Husband, Richard Ratzlaff, Ian MacKenzie, and the rest of the staff at the University of Toronto Press for expertly seeing the project through to publication.

Finally, I want to express my gratitude to the talented cast and crew – especially Joan Bryans, the director – who brought these words brilliantly to life onstage at the University of British Columbia Chan Centre for the Performing Arts. The fact that works written over two thousand years ago can still be successfully performed today tells us a great deal about our shared humanity across the ages.

Furry Creek, British Columbia
July 2007

# Introduction

More than 2,400 years after his death, Socrates remains an iconic but controversial figure. According to his supporters, he personified progressive Greek ideals of justice, wisdom, and temperance. According to his detractors, he was a corruptor of the young and one of the reasons Athens suffered its humiliating defeat by Sparta in 404 BCE,[1] twenty-seven years after the outbreak of the second Peloponnesian War.

Some of the most striking accounts discussing this period are contained in the writings of three of Socrates' contemporaries: the playwright Aristophanes, the philosopher Plato, and the military general Xenophon. All three authors knew Socrates personally and all three help us understand not only the times in which he lived but also the important events that shaped his life.

Aristophanes' slapstick comedy, *Clouds*, was first performed in 423 BCE, eight years after the outbreak of war between Athens and Sparta. It tells the story of how, instead of being educated, a young man named Pheidippides is corrupted by Socrates and the changing educational standards of his day. The play's premiere is reported to have taken place in front of a capacity crowd of 17,000 and Socrates himself is said to have attended. Even so, the play came only third in the Dionysia, the main annual dramatic competition in Athens. This may have been because it was ahead of its time: *Clouds* is one of the first Greek comedies to contain what we now call a plot. Earlier plays within what scholars refer to as the Old Comedy were typically little more than compilations of what have often been called 'dick and fart jokes.'[2]

Almost a quarter century after Aristophanes' play appeared, Socrates was brought to trial on charges of corrupting the young and failing to honour the traditional Greek gods. He was found guilty and sentenced to death. Today, two versions of the speech he gave at his trial survive. One is by Plato. The other is by Xenophon. Both present a strikingly different portrait of Socrates from the one given to us by Aristophanes. In Plato's *Apology* and again in Xenophon's *Defence*,[3] Socrates emphatically denies the charges being brought against him. He explains to the jury that he believes in the same gods they do and that he has not been a corrupter of the young. Of course, history has nowhere recorded word-for-word versions of any of the speeches made at Socrates' trial. Even so, Aristophanes has given us a credible portrayal of the case that was likely offered by the prosecution, just as Plato and Xenophon have recorded plausible summaries of the case Socrates no doubt put forward in his own defence.

In addition to these works, two other dialogues by Plato are especially helpful for understanding the events surrounding Socrates' trial. In the *Crito* and the *Phaedo*, Socrates discusses the jury's verdict and talks about his forthcoming execution. He explains why he is not frightened of death and why he thinks it important to obey the law, even when it goes against one's immediate interests. The *Phaedo* ends with Plato's dramatic recounting of one of the most famous death scenes in all history.

The following script is an adaptation of Aristophanes' *Clouds* and Plato's *Apology, Crito,* and *Phaedo*. It tells the story of Socrates' trial and execution in modern language and is intended to appeal to contemporary audiences.

Socrates lived in the Greek city state of Athens from about 469 to 399 BCE. His life and the lives of his followers were closely connected to the rise of Greek philosophy, law, science, and democracy.

Attempts to discover the historical Socrates are hindered by the fact that he wrote nothing.[4] Everything known about him comes from the writings of others. These include Aristophanes' play, a series of dialogues by Plato, several quite different accounts by Xenophon, and a number of secondhand reports by ancient philosophers and historians such as Aristotle, Aeschines, Cicero, and Diogenes Laertius. Although references can be found to many other ancient authors who mention or discuss Socrates – including Hermogenes, Simon the cobbler, Alexamenos of Teos, at least nine of the eighteen Socratics named by Plato in the *Phaedo*, and at least four comic playwrights in addition to Aristophanes – none of their works have survived. Unfortunately too, the accounts that have survived are not always consistent. For example, although Plato and Xenophon both knew Socrates personally, their reports of Socrates' defence speech and of the man himself differ in important ways. The Socrates described by Xenophon – who Diogenes Laertius tells us was the first to record his recollections,[5] even though Xenophon himself also tells us that others had previously written about Socrates and his trial[6] – is often taken to be little more than a common-sense moralist, someone who provides guidance to young men before they take their place in society. In contrast, Plato's Socrates is full of humour and irony. He is equally at home among the most- and least-privileged members of Athenian society and he clearly recognizes the influence he has had on the city of Athens as a whole. In Plato's dialogues we encounter a profound thinker, someone acquainted with the highest learning of his day.[7]

Our understanding of this period of history is also complicated by the fact that although Xenophon wrote primarily as a historian, this isn't true of many other ancient authors. Aristophanes of course wrote primarily for entertainment and, although the purpose of Plato's writings is less clear, it's likely he intended his dialogues to serve both dramatic and philosophical purposes as much as historical ones. Because Plato also wrote over such a long period of time, it's also likely that his later dialogues had purposes different from those of his earlier ones.[8] Even so, by looking for points of overlap among various historical documents and by exercising careful scholarly judgement, many details of Socrates' life can be reconstructed with reasonable certainty.

In 469 BCE, the year Socrates was born, Athens was full of energy and new ideas. Two decades earlier, the Athenian army had defeated the much stronger Persian army at the famous Battle of Marathon. Legend has it that a soldier ran all the way from Marathon to Athens without stopping, a distance of about thirty-four kilometres (or twenty-one miles), to report news of the victory. Immediately after delivering the news, he is said to have dropped dead from exhaustion.[9]

Although the story is of uncertain authenticity – for example, the ancient historian Herodotus tells only of a runner being sent from Marathon to Sparta and back in a futile attempt to enlist the Spartans in the upcoming battle, a much greater distance[10] – winning the Battle of Marathon gave Athens tremendous confidence in itself. Athenian ships began to travel the Mediterranean and international trade became common. The position of Athens as head of the Delian League (the major military alliance of Greece), together with the discovery of silver, turned Socrates' hometown into a prosperous city.[11] When Socrates was a child, the future Athenian leader Pericles was also a young man.[12] As Socrates and Pericles matured, so did Athens. By the time Socrates was twenty, Athens had become a rich, cosmopolitan city and the undisputed centre of the Greek world.

It was during this same century that Athens began experimenting with a radical new form of government. Advocates of this new form of government originally called it an *isonomy*, meaning 'equality under the law.' As the Persian nobleman Otanes is reported to have said when attempting to convince his countrymen to adopt this new type of government,

> The rule of the majority has the most beautiful name of all: equality under the law [isonomy] ... The holders of magistracies are selected by lot and are held accountable for their actions. All deliberations are in public. I predict that we will give up monarchy and replace it with democracy. For in democracy all things are possible.[13]

The second name for this new form of government, *democracy*, meant something close to 'mob rule' and came from the Greek words *demos* meaning 'people' and *kratos* meaning 'power.' Eventually, it was this second name that became universal. As we read in Thucydides' report of Pericles' famous *Funeral Oration*, delivered just prior to the outbreak of the second Peloponnesian War,

> Our constitution is called a 'democracy' because power is in the hands, not of a minority, but of the whole people. When it is a question of settling private disputes, everyone is equal before the law; when it is a question of putting one person before another in positions of public responsibility, what counts is not membership of a particular class, but the actual ability the man possesses. No one, so long as he has it in him to be of service to the state, is kept in political obscurity because of poverty.[14]

Although slavery was still common and only free adult men born of Athenian parents could become voting citizens, this new form of government represented a radical departure from the many tyrannies and oligarchies that had traditionally ruled Greek city states.

When Socrates was about twenty-one, the Athenians, under the leadership of Pericles, began constructing Greece's most famous building, the Parthenon. The project took more than a decade to complete. Once finished, it was one of the grandest structures ever seen. Perched atop the Acropolis, the highest hill in Athens, the Parthenon soon came to symbolize everything that was central to being Athenian.

Although little is known about Socrates' parents, it is possible that his father was one of the sculptors, or perhaps a stonemason, who worked on the Parthenon.[15] His mother appears to have been a midwife.[16] Like other boys in Athens, Socrates probably received a classical education involving the study of music, gymnastics, and grammar.[17] He was also exposed to the developing science and mathematics of his day.[18] Together, all such disciplines were beginning to be known as *philosophy*, meaning 'love of wisdom.'

According to some reports, as a young man Socrates became interested in the cause of eclipses. He also became interested in the debate between two groups: the Milesians,[19] who said the earth was flat, and the Italians, who said it was spherical. It is even possible that he was introduced to the question of whether all mathematical properties could be described using the whole numbers (1, 2, 3, ... ) or whether other kinds of numbers (such as the real numbers) were also necessary. Later he abandoned these topics, becoming more interested in questions about how best to live one's life, including questions about the nature of right and wrong. As the Roman writer Cicero tells us, it is for this reason that Socrates was said to have 'called philosophy down from heaven, settled it in cities, introduced it into houses and made it necessary for inquiries to be made on life and morals, good and evil.'[20] As Socrates saw it, human happiness (or flourishing)[21] required a detailed understanding of the cardinal virtues of courage, temperance, justice, piety, and wisdom. In other words, according to Socrates, being committed to virtue (or excellence)[22] is necessary for anyone wanting to live a good life.[23]

Between the ages of about twenty and fifty, Socrates periodically served as a hoplite, or armed foot soldier, in the Athenian army. This service became especially important following the outbreak of war in 431 BCE.[24] During a particularly sharp skirmish at Potidaea, a young Athenian soldier named Alcibiades was wounded. Seeing this, Socrates threw himself between Alcibiades and his attackers, saving his life.[25] Later, when the Athenians found themselves retreating from their disastrous campaign at Delium, Alcibiades was able to return the favour. Now of higher rank and on horseback, he refused to abandon Socrates, who was again fighting on foot, remaining with him until they were both safe from danger.[26] Despite their differences – Alcibiades was rich and handsome, and famous for his extravagance and self-indulgence, while Socrates was poor and physically unattractive, and famous for his self-discipline – the two men appear to have remained lifelong friends, with Socrates periodically serving as a sort of mentor to the younger man.

This type of mentoring relationship was something of an institution in ancient Greece and sometimes involved an intimate as well as an educational component. Especially among the wealthy, temporary relationships between adult males (or *erastai* meaning 'lovers') and young men (or *eromenoi*, literally the 'recipients of love') were common, although not universal. These relationships were the subject of debate – for example, Plato was against the practice – and were distinct from both marriage and homosexual partnerships, the latter of which were often looked down upon but also often tolerated with a wink, provided they didn't violate the bounds of common decorum.[27]

According to one tradition, although Socrates was no different from his contemporaries in finding young men attractive,[28] he was unlike other mentors in that he was determined to keep his mentoring relationships independent of sexual involvement.[29] If this is correct, it is unlikely that the charge of corrupting the young would have involved a sexual component. Even so, more than two millennia after the fact, and with less than complete evidence to go on, it is difficult to know this with certainty. It may even be that, in the minds of some jurors, it was the *absence* of an intimate relationship that was inappropriate, since this might have been thought akin to having influence over the young without responsibility.[30] In any event, this aspect of Greek life should not be overlooked even if, as seems most likely, it had little or nothing to do with the charges that were eventually brought against Socrates. What is clear is that, among the young, Socrates was a popular and influential figure and it was partly through Alcibiades' family connections that Socrates became known to the political and military elites of Athens. So important was Alcibiades' family that, after Alcibiades' father had been killed in battle years earlier, it was Pericles himself who had been appointed Alcibiades' guardian.

Within the Athenian aristocracy, Socrates soon became both famous and infamous. Those who knew him respected him because of his war record. They also tell us that he was intelligent, self-disciplined, and fun to be around. Although he may have worked occasionally as a stonemason, between his periods of military service he spent most of his time in the agora, or marketplace, and in the gymnasiums, talking and arguing with anyone who would join him in debate. Sitting barefoot[31] outside the cobbler's shop[32] in the shadow of the Acropolis, Socrates saw it as his role to goad his fellow citizens out of their moral and intellectual complacency. Comparing himself to a 'gadfly'[33] (or large horsefly) and his fellow citizens to a slow, dim-witted horse, Socrates was widely recognized for his provocative comments and sharp tongue.

Because Athens was a democracy, public speaking was an important skill for all citizens. By all accounts, Socrates was an especially effective public speaker. Since many young men enjoyed listening to him speak, some people confused him with other men called *sophists* (literally 'wise men') who earned their living giving young people practical instruction in argument and rhetoric. One of the most famous of the sophists was Protagoras. For a fee, he would teach people how to argue for or against any position. As a result, he became notorious for his ability to make the weaker argument appear to be the stronger. His book (or more precisely, scroll), entitled *Truth*, was nicknamed *The Throws*. Like a good wrestling coach, it taught his students how to overthrow other people's arguments. In his book, Protagoras argued that 'man is the measure of all things' and that there is no such thing as objective truth.[34] In other words, according to Protagoras, since all beliefs are subjective, it follows that effective arguments can be found in favour of, or against, any position whatsoever!

Plato tells us that, in contrast to teachers like Protagoras, Socrates took no money for his teaching and argued only in favour of propositions that seemed to him to be true. According to legend, he also always won his arguments with the sophists.[35] Whether this was true or not, Protagoras and the other professional teachers could not have been too pleased to be upstaged in public by someone whose followers were learning how to think and argue for free.

Ancient sources report that Socrates was not handsome.[36] He was not tall and he had prominent eyes and a snub nose. These same authors also tell us that he was physically strong and brave and had all the other qualities that make a good soldier. In late middle age, he appears to have married a younger woman named Xanthippe. Although Xanthippe is traditionally reported to have been a shrew,[37] it's likely that she was just as fond of Socrates as he was of her.[38] One (possibly spurious) letter even goes so far as to reprimand her for her prolonged mourning following Socrates' death.[39] Even so, details about Socrates' family life are difficult to establish with much certainty. For example, it may be that Xanthippe was Socrates' first wife and that he later married another woman named Myrto.[40] More likely, Xanthippe was his second wife, his first wife having died of the plague.[41] It is even possible that during this period, because so many men had died in the war, the men who remained were being encouraged to take two wives to help re-establish the city's male population.[42] Socrates is also traditionally reported to have been the father of three sons, Lamprokles, Sophroniskos, and Menexenos, at most one of whom had reached the age of majority by the time of their father's trial, although even here the historical record is less than complete.[43] In any event, not being interested in money, Socrates earned only enough to get by. Summer or winter, he wore no sandals and the same threadbare cloak. As one acquaintance, the sophist Antiphon, is reported to have said, 'Even a slave who was made to live this way would run away!'[44] Given his spartan lifestyle, and his apparent lack of interest in providing for his family, it is likely that Xanthippe had good reason to worry and complain.

Eventually Socrates' fame began to spread beyond his home city. Northwest of Athens was the famous town of Delphi. Here, high on the slopes of Mount Parnassus in a landscape of indescribable beauty, athletes from all over Greece came to participate in the Pythian Games. The Games were part of a four-year cycle known as the Olympiad, or Panhellenic Games, that consisted of the Olympic Games, the Nemean Games, the Pythian Games, and the Isthmian Games. Held two years before (and two years after) each Olympic Games, the Pythian Games were organized to honour Apollo, the god of prophecy. They involved not just athletic competitions but also competitions in music and poetry. A three-month truce during times of war even permitted soldiers from opposing armies to compete against one another. Winners were awarded laurel wreaths and became famous throughout Greece.[45]

Just as importantly, Delphi was a place where people were said to be able to communicate with Apollo. In return for payments of various kinds, a priestess (known as the Pythian) would forecast the future. The priestess and the temple where she resided were together known as Delphic Oracle. As Plutarch tells us, the Delphic Oracle was 'the most ancient in time and the most famous in repute' of all the Greek oracles.[46]

One famous prediction by the Oracle concerned King Croesus of Lydia, in Asia Minor. The king wanted to know whether he should risk continuing his war against the Persians. In response to his question, the Oracle told him that if he continued the war, a great empire would fall. Predictions by the Oracle were regularly made in this kind of ambiguous language, making it difficult to prove them wrong. Thinking the prediction meant he would defeat the Persians, the king made the decision to enter into battle. Unfortunately for him, the great empire that was defeated was his own.[47]

Because of Socrates' growing reputation for being wise, a friend of Socrates named Chaerephon asked the Oracle if anyone was wiser than the Athenian philosopher.[48] The Oracle's answer was uncharacteristically clear: among all men, Socrates was the wisest.[49] When told of this, Socrates was puzzled. Despite his respect for the Oracle, he found it difficult to accept the suggestion that he was especially wise. As a result, he began to wonder whether, despite its straightforward appearance, the Oracle's answer might really have been some kind of riddle. What exactly was the Oracle trying to say? What did it mean to be wise?

Uncertain of what the Oracle could have meant, and thinking he might be able to disprove the straightforward meaning of the prophecy, Socrates began searching for someone who was wiser than he was. In the centre of Athens near the tables of the moneylenders, he began trying to unravel the mystery of how anyone – let alone a god – could think he was the wisest of all men.

This public mission to test the Oracle's prophecy occupied Socrates for many years but brought him only poverty and hardship. As he questioned his fellow Athenians, he discovered that many who claimed to be wise were unable to give a coherent account of why they believed what they did. As a result, Socrates eventually came to the conclusion that the Oracle may have been right after all: although other people thought they were wise when really they weren't, at least he knew he wasn't wise. In this comparative sense, perhaps he was even the wisest of all men!

In carrying out his mission to test the Oracle's pronouncement, Socrates must have annoyed many people who thought highly of themselves, just as he had annoyed Protagoras and the sophists. At the same time, his jokes and arguments would certainly have entertained the many onlookers who gathered around to listen, including many of the younger members of Athenian aristocracy. It is likely that this was part of what eventually led to charges being brought against him, since it was some of these same young men who later attempted to overthrow the democracy that had served Athens so well for so long.[50]

It was in this context that Socrates also began questioning the nature and role of the traditional Greek gods.[51] Is an action right because some authority (for example, a god) commands it? Or should an authority command an action because it is right? If the former, why would the gods' mere preference make something right? If the latter, then the action will be right, and we should do it, regardless of whether it is commanded. In either case, what need is there for the command? What need is there for the gods?[52]

The outrage that these kinds of remarks must have caused is not surprising. During their life-and-death struggle with Sparta, almost all Athenians would have recognized that the two most important requirements for victory were the protection of the gods and the unwavering loyalty of a city's young soldiers. To undermine such protections during times of war would have been widely recognized as a kind of sedition.

Even so, the exact nature of Socrates' growing influence remained a matter of controversy. According to his accusers, Socrates was responsible for introducing a toxic blend of ethical relativism, epistemic scepticism, and religious non-conformism. In contrast, according to Plato and Xenophon, Socrates simply saw it as his duty to remind his fellow citizens of the difference between right and wrong, good and bad, and to help them test themselves (and each other) against a series of ideal virtues. Just as a marksman needs a target at which to aim, people need to know how to distinguish right from wrong if they are to lead good lives. As Socrates famously put it, 'The unexamined life is not worth living.'[53]

Among the many other questions Socrates raised with his followers were questions about the nature of justice, truth, and friendship. It's because he often claimed not to know the answers to such questions that he is sometimes thought to have been a sceptic, someone who believes that it is impossible to acquire knowledge. However, this interpretation is clearly mistaken. Despite his assertion that he was not wise, Socrates did not think knowledge was impossible to obtain. Not only did he claim to know that the unexamined life is not worth living, he also claimed to know that excellence and virtue are identical to knowledge, and that it is only out of ignorance that we do evil. He claimed to know that since a person's character can be damaged only by doing injustice, it's better to be treated unjustly than to commit an immoral act, and that since harm to one's body is not as important as harm to one's character, death should not be seen as an evil. In other words, a man of good character can never truly be harmed.[54]

Socrates also regularly told his listeners that he knew there were many things he didn't know. The reason he sometimes also paradoxically said he knew nothing was that, for him, genuine knowledge came only with thorough understanding.[55] For Socrates and his followers, a few disjointed beliefs, even if they were true and well supported, did not count as genuine knowledge or, as we might better say, wisdom.

Even so, judging by the writings of Plato, Xenophon, and others, Socrates' influence on his followers, both before and after his death, was considerable. In large part this was because of the originality of his views. As Aristotle sums up, Socrates' views 'are never commonplace: they always exhibit a grace and originality of thought' not found in the views of others.[56]

In 399 BCE, Socrates was brought to trial on charges of corrupting the young and failing to recognize the traditional Greek gods. As Plato reports the indictment, 'Socrates is guilty of corrupting the young and of not believing in the gods in whom the city believes, but in other new spiritual things.'[57] As Xenophon records it, Socrates was accused of 'not acknowledging the gods the city acknowledged, of introducing new daimonic activities instead and corrupting the young';[58] and as Diogenes Laertius repeats the charges, Socrates was 'guilty of refusing to recognize the gods recognized by the state, and of introducing other new divinities. He is also guilty of corrupting the young.'[59]

Most likely there was a connection between the charges. The most natural way of reading them is that it was because of Socrates' religious non-conformism that he was believed to have been a corrupting influence on the young.[60] Whether this was true or not, there is also reason to think there may have been a political motive behind the legal action. In a society in which religion and politics were so closely intertwined, it is likely that a charge of religious non-conformism would itself have had political overtones.

At the time of Socrates' trial, the long war between Athens and Sparta had been over for only five years. Socrates himself was now seventy and the city where he had lived all his life had changed over the years. Pericles was dead and the war had left Athens tired and less prosperous. Several of Socrates' friends and followers – including Alcibiades and two of Plato's relatives – had been involved in a series of treasonous acts. Plato's cousin Critias and his uncle Charmides had been among those who had attempted to overthrow the democratic government of the day and substitute in its place an oligarchy. Before defecting to Sparta, Alcibiades had also likely been responsible for the sacrilegious mutilation of a large number of popular religious statues called *herms* – the statues were ithyphallic and many had had their phalluses broken off[61] – and after his defection he had given the Spartans invaluable advice about how best to take advantage of weaknesses in Athenian defences.

Because of these events, many Athenians had become suspicious of new ideas and of dissent. Many people believed that, to lose the war, Athens must have offended the city's protector, the goddess Athena, and that men such as Critias and Alcibiades must have been inappropriately indoctrinated by their teachers. It was in this context that Socrates was charged and found guilty. The three men who made the charges were Meletus, Anytus, and Lykon.

In Socrates' day, juries could range in size from a few hundred to several thousand citizens. The exact size of Socrates' jury is unknown, although similar trials appear sometimes to have used juries of 500 (or later 501) jurors. Plato tells us only that Socrates addressed his remarks to a sizeable number of jurors,[62] that the case was lost by a relatively small margin,[63] and that if thirty of those who voted for conviction had instead voted for acquittal the decision would have been reversed,[64] a number that is difficult to make consistent with the (admittedly much later) account given by Diogenes Laertius.[65] Xenophon makes no mention of the number of jurors.

In any event, given their large number, different jurors likely had different reasons for supporting conviction. Some jurors may genuinely have wanted Socrates to be convicted for impiety. Others may have been convinced that he was a corrosive influence on the young, not so much because of his impiety but simply because he had spent so much time challenging the moral and intellectual complacency of his fellow citizens. Others appear to have been put off by the confrontational manner in which he delivered his defence speech. Still others may simply have been willing to go along with the crowd. In any case, because the first amnesty in recorded history had been announced, charges against wartime traitors could not be made openly.[66] This would have given some people an incentive to look for more indirect causes of the city's disastrous loss to Sparta. It would also have meant that supporters of traitors like Alcibiades would have to be charged with crimes other than treason if they were ever to be brought to justice.

Judging from the evidence available today, it appears unlikely that Socrates would have supported the anti-democratic uprisings that took place towards the end of the Peloponnesian War. If Plato's writings are reliable on this point, Socrates appears to have been at least as supportive of the democrats as of the oligarchs, and possibly more so.[67] Unlike Plato and Xenophon, and unlike the Socrates character Plato uses in many of his later writings, including his famous *Republic*, the historical Socrates appears to have been in favour of many of the most important principles underlying Athenian democracy. He also appears to have been no friend of the anti-democrats: while in power, Critias and the other tyrants tried to reduce Socrates' influence by forbidding him from speaking to any man under thirty.[68] Even so, if Xenophon is correct, a case still needed to be made defending him against the view that he had been responsible for educating some of the city's most notorious traitors.[69] Because banishment was a common form of punishment during this period, many people may have hoped that the charges would force Socrates to leave Athens.

Among scholars there remains debate over exactly where Socrates' trial took place.[70] In Athens there were several law courts, each having a different purpose.[71] Trials at some of these courts were held indoors. Others were held outdoors. Trials at the Heliaia, the oldest and most senior court in Athens, appear to have been held inside a walled courtyard, with the wall likely high enough to separate members of the jury from the general public, but low enough to allow spectators outside the courtyard to observe the proceedings. Originally a hedge rather than a wall may have separated the courtyard from the rest of the agora.

Because charges of impiety fell under the jurisdiction of the King Archon (or chief magistrate), initial depositions in Socrates' case appear to have been taken at the Royal Stoa (or Stoa Basileios) at the north end of the agora.[72] However, the trial itself would likely have been held elsewhere, probably at the Heliaia. Alternatively, it may have been held at the Areopagus (literally the 'Hill of Ares') at the south end of the agora near the foot of the Acropolis. It was on this rocky outcropping that cases of intentional homicide, wounding, poisoning, and arson had originally been tried, allowing the religious 'pollution' associated with such crimes to be dissipated into the open air. Cases of impiety may also have been held here, again so that their 'pollution' would avoid contaminating the city's agora and temples.

Originally the Areopagus had also served as the main public meeting place for members of the city's fledging democracy. Later, growth in the city's population led to the reforms of Ephialtes (around 462 BCE) and meetings of the Assembly moved to a larger hill, the Pnyx. The Areopagus thus began to play a much less central role, although in Socrates' day it may still have been used as the site for some public meetings and trials. If Socrates' trial was held at the Areopagus rather than in the Heliaia, the jury likely would have been sequestered by a rope dipped in red dye. Anyone attempting to enter or leave the jury area would have been stained by the dye – a sure sign of impropriety. Wherever the trial was held, the space had to be large enough to hold at least some members of the general public as well as the jury and court officials.

In Socrates' day, trials followed a specific format. After the charges were read, the accuser spoke. He explained why the defendant ought to be found guilty. Then the defendant spoke. He explained why he ought to be found innocent. Both sides could invite others to provide evidence or speak on their behalf.[73] All speeches were timed with a water clock to ensure that equal time was given to the prosecution and the defence.[74] Immediately after the speeches, the jury gave its verdict. If the accuser received fewer than one-fifth the total number of votes, he was fined for making a frivolous charge.[75] If the defendant received fewer than half the total number of votes, he was found guilty. If there was no penalty fixed by law – as in Socrates' case – both sides were required to propose a punishment. The jury then chose between the two proposals. The fact that there was no possibility of compromise was intended to motivate both sides to suggest reasonable penalties.[76]

Socrates treated the whole affair with good-natured contempt, teasing Meletus and the others about how silly their charges were. In his own defence, he pointed out that over the years he had been a critic of both the democrats *and* the anti-democrats. As many people knew, when the democrats had been in power several years earlier, Socrates had stood alone in opposing an unconstitutional motion condemning a group of army generals who had been charged collectively (rather than individually) with abandoning their shipwrecked colleagues in the midst of the Battle of Arginusae, the largest sea battle of the Peloponnesian War.[77] Two years later, when the anti-democrats were in power, he had refused to obey an illegal order given by Plato's cousin, Critias, to participate in the arrest of an innocent man.[78] Either action could easily have cost Socrates his life. As Socrates told the jury, the lesson he drew from these events was that, had he participated in the day-to-day politics of Athens any more than he had, he surely would have been put to death much sooner.[79]

Although Socrates regularly questioned the established religion of his day, he also told the jury that in every important respect he was an ordinary religious man who did his best to honour the gods of the city. He took great pride in pointing out that Aristophanes' well-known caricature of him as a sophist with his head in the clouds was mistaken.[80]

Following the speeches, the vote appears to have been a close one, but Socrates was found guilty. Meletus requested the death sentence. In reply, Socrates told the jury that what he really deserved was to be given free meals for life at the Prytaneum (the Athenian equivalent of the modern city hall) to thank him for the many services he had provided his fellow citizens over the years![81] Such support was given only to the city's most distinguished war heroes, Olympians, and public benefactors. Realizing that the jury would not accept this rather humorous suggestion, Socrates canvassed a number of more plausible counterproposals, including exile and prison. Eventually he told the jury that he would be willing to pay a small fine. The amount he initially proposed has traditionally been reported as being one silver mina (the equivalent of 100 drachmas),[82] or perhaps less,[83] since this was all he could afford. At the urging of his followers he increased this to thirty minas (or 3,000 drachmas), to be paid by several of his supporters, including his lifelong friend Crito, one of the richest men in Athens.[84] Unlike the smaller fine, 3,000 drachmas would have been a significant sum, even for a prosperous person.[85] However, provoked by Socrates' initial claim that he saw himself as one of the city's greatest benefactors, the jury sentenced him to death instead.

Following the sentencing, Socrates gave a final series of impromptu remarks that many jury members likely stayed to hear. In these remarks Socrates admitted that many people might have preferred to hear him give a more conciliatory, apologetic speech. However, he told his listeners that such a speech would not have been appropriate for him or the city. Despite the fact that he had been sentenced to death, he told the jury that it simply would not have been right for him to beg for his life. He also admitted that since childhood he believed he had been accompanied by a daimonion, a small voice or sign that he understood to have originated from one of the gods.[86] This voice or sign warned him whenever he was about to do something wrong or harmful. Because there had been no voice or sign warning him against giving his speech, Socrates understood this to be a 'great proof' that he had done the right thing in speaking plainly – almost confrontationally – to the jury.[87]

Although executions in Athens usually took place within twenty-four hours, Socrates' execution was delayed a month for religious reasons. Every spring the city sent an offering to the island of Delos to honour the god Apollo. To maintain ritual purity, executions weren't permitted until a ship returned with word that the offering had been accepted. During this time, Crito offered to help Socrates escape from

prison and smuggle him out of Athens.[88] Socrates refused. Since he had
lived willingly as a citizen under the laws of Athens all his life and since
he had accepted the many benefits these laws gave him, he believed he
needed to accept their less welcome consequences as well. The arguments Socrates gave in support of this view are the first in recorded history in favour of a secular social-contract theory.[89] Having just told all
of Athens that he was not responsible for corrupting the young, he also
wanted to show his fellow citizens that he had not lied. In effect, he was
telling his supporters that he was willing to stand by his principles and
serve as a role model to the young, even if this meant death.

To fulfil the order of execution, Socrates was required to drink a cup
of hemlock, a type of poison. His last words after the hemlock had
begun to do its work were that he and his friends owed a debt to Asclepius, the god of medicine. Exactly why they owed this debt is not
made clear. One explanation – among the many sometimes given by
commentators – is that Socrates was indicating a concern for the health
of his soul as he was about to enter the afterlife. A second suggestion is
that since Plato was at home recovering from an illness, the offering
was meant to give thanks for Plato's improving health. A third is that
the comment was just one more instance of Socrates' famous sense of
humour – that, in effect, he was thanking the god for such efficient poison! A fourth – and most likely – is that the offering was simply part of
an annual religious festival that, among other things, recognized the
debt all Athenians owed to Asclepius for having delivered them some
years earlier from the plague.[90] Having just argued in front of all of
Athens that he respected the gods of the city and that he was not a corruptor of the young, Socrates would have been particularly concerned
to observe the appropriate rituals. One way of making such an offering
was by sacrificing a bird or small animal: 'Crito,' he said to his friend,
'we owe a rooster to Asclepius. Pay the debt, and don't forget.'[91]

Legend has it that not long after Socrates' execution, the citizens of
Athens felt such remorse that they killed Meletus and banished Anytus
and Lykon. Some years later they also may have honoured Socrates by
placing a bronze statue of him in the city's Hall of Processions.[92]
According to some historians, such legends are of questionable authenticity but, whether factual or not, Socrates' influence on his fellow Athenians could hardly have been greater. This same influence continues to
be felt over two thousand years later.[93]

The following script presents the central features of Socrates' story as
given to us by Aristophanes, Plato, and other classical Greek authors.

In developing the script, the intention has not been to provide audiences with a word-for-word translation of any specific Greek text or texts. Instead, it has been to emphasize the central storyline found in the works of these authors while at the same time providing audiences with a unified narrative that fits comfortably in the space of a single theatrical performance. Although fresh language has been used throughout – only a very few historically important passages remain exactly as originally written – the script still attempts to remain faithful to the general tenor and tone of the primary texts. Even so, many scenes have been significantly shortened and all three acts borrow freely from other ancient sources, as well as from the playwright's imagination. For example, it is in Aristotle (and not in Plato or Aristophanes) that we find Socrates' famous line, 'The difficulty is not to praise the Athenians at Athens but at Sparta.'[94] It is in Aelian that Socrates observes that tragedy is more likely to accompany the lives of great men than those of more common people – such as members of the Chorus.[95] It is in Xenophon that we learn that when offered the chance to escape, Socrates responded by asking his friends 'whether they knew of some place outside Attica not accessible to death.'[96] These and similar lines have been paraphrased and inserted without attribution whenever they have added to the script's overall dramatic effect.

In act 1, almost all parts of Aristophanes' original play not pertaining to Socrates have been omitted. This has been done partly for reasons of length, partly because it is only these features of the storyline that are relevant to current dramatic purposes, and partly because the only extant version of Aristophanes' play is itself merely a partially revised version of the original. In addition, the current script contains very little of Aristophanes' original Chorus. No literal translation can be faithful to Aristophanes' words and, at the same time, successfully convey the cadence and vitality of the original Greek. Since the primary purpose of any play is to entertain, the current Chorus honours the playwright's intentions rather than his words. Unashamedly, pizzazz has been preferred to pedantry. Directors and other readers wanting to revisit Aristophanes' original language may do so using any number of reliable translations.

In the case of Xanthippe, only a very limited amount of dialogue is given in ancient sources. All of it is controversial. For example, the anecdote in which Xanthippe complains that she requires better food if she is to entertain guests appears only in Diogenes Laertius, writing several hundred years after these events took place.[97] Whether he was relying upon written texts now lost or merely upon oral tradition is not known.

Similarly, although the flamboyant businessman Apollodorus is traditionally reported to have commented that he would find it especially
hard to see Socrates being put to death unjustly[98] – prompting Socrates
to ask whether he would prefer to see him being put to death *justly* –
there is a separate tradition again stemming from Diogenes that assigns
this role to Xanthippe.[99] Although scholars will want to debate which
tradition is the more authoritative, the current script is content simply to
tell an exciting story. Additional wording has been inspired from other
contexts. For example, Socrates' suggestion that he might escape some
night, hiding under an old goatskin cloak as if he were a criminal,
appears to have been made originally to Crito, not Xanthippe,[100] but
having made the comment to one person, it is perhaps not unlikely that
he also would have made it to others, including his wife.[101]

On the important issue of whether the charges brought against
Socrates were primarily religious, primarily educational, or primarily
political, the current script is content to steer a middle course, believing
that during Socrates' day such concerns would have been largely indis-
tinguishable in the minds of most jurors. Because victory in war was
understood to require the blessing of the gods, teaching disrespect for
the gods would naturally have been understood as a type of sedition. So
although Plato makes no mention of the political nature of the charges,
both Aeschines and Xenophon explicitly name Socrates as the teacher of
Critias and Alcibiades, leading us to infer that it was because of
Socrates' influence on these men that Athens lost the war to Sparta.[102]

In the case of Socrates' death scene, while Plato provides the scaffold-
ing, the building materials have again come from a variety of sources.
For example, one of the executioners, a public slave, is reported to have
said of Socrates that he was 'the noblest, the gentlest, and the best' of all
the men he ever encountered.[103] Phaedo, a friend and former slave, ech-
oed this remark, saying that Socrates was 'the best and wisest and most
righteous of men.'[104] Years after the event, Xenophon tells us that if
anyone who seeks virtue ever meets with any more agreeable companion than Socrates, he would 'consider him worthy of being called the
most blessed of all.'[105] The current script allows Crito to sum up all
three of these reports as follows: 'Then it's time to say goodbye, and let
history record these words: Of all the men I've known, he was by far the
wisest, most virtuous, and best.' It is hoped that these and other adap-
tations help make the storyline accessible to contemporary audiences.
The goal throughout has been to develop language that is as informative as it is entertaining and as entertaining as it is informative.

Socrates' story is rightly one of historic proportions. During a time of war and great social and intellectual upheaval, Socrates felt compelled to express his views openly, regardless of the consequences. As a result, he is remembered today, not only for his sharp wit and high ethical standards, but also for his loyalty to the view that in a democracy the best way for a man to serve himself, his friends, and his city – even during times of war – is by being loyal to, and by speaking publicly about, the truth. This idea was controversial during Socrates' time.[106] It remains controversial to the present day.

# Production Notes

This play brings together abbreviated, adapted versions of Aristophanes' *Clouds* and Plato's *Apology, Crito,* and *Phaedo.* The play has been designed to appeal to modern audiences.

The script is in three acts. The first emphasizes many of the most humorous scenes in Aristophanes' original stage play. The second and third acts are more dramatic, although they too contain moments of clear comedy. All three acts follow the original texts closely but not slavishly. It is the purpose of act 1 to help contextualize Socrates' defence speech in act 2 and to give audiences an understanding of why the charge of corrupting the young might plausibly have been raised against the Athenian philosopher. The third act, which serves as the play's denouement, has intentionally been kept short.

The script allows for audience participation in two ways. The first is that during the second act, audience members are invited to join in heckling Socrates. As Plato tells us, Athenian juries were often 'noisy and disorderly as though they were in a theatre, clapping or hooting at the speaker on either side in turn.'[1] To assist them, it is helpful if cast members playing the role of Hecklers can be scattered discreetly throughout the house.

The second place for audience participation also occurs in act 2, when audience members are encouraged to play the role of jurors and vote in favour of Socrates' guilt or innocence. One effective way of doing this is to have audience members walk to the front of the theatre to choose either a black or white stone and place it in a bronze container.[2] Voting by a public show of hands – which was common in Athenian assemblies, but rare in Athenian trials – is not recommended, since a persuasive performance on the part of the actor playing the role of

Socrates will often encourage more audience members to vote in favour of acquittal than history allows.

In large theatres, directors may choose to restrict the size of the jury. However, given the large size of Athenian juries (often 500 jurors or more), it is more realistic to use larger rather than smaller portions of the audience for this purpose. Experience also shows that participating as jurors is something that audience members enjoy.

One point of historical departure is that the current script gives the jury only a single opportunity to vote. Originally two votes were taken: the first to determine Socrates' guilt or innocence, the second to choose between proposed penalties after he was found guilty.[3] In contexts requiring greater historical authenticity, this second vote can easily be reintroduced although, depending on the size of the jury, doing so may add significantly to the act's running time.

Because the final act is comparatively short, and because audience members will have had a chance to stretch their legs during the voting near the end of act 2 as well as in the intermission at the end of act 1, a second intermission will not normally be required.

In casting, different actors are to be assigned the role of Socrates in act 1 and act 2. The same actor is to be assigned this role in act 2 and act 3. Not only do the second and third acts take place twenty-four years after the first act, the Socrates of the first act is merely an actor representing the Socrates of the later two acts.

According to the Roman rhetoritician Aelian, Socrates himself attended the premiere of *Clouds* in 423 BCE and so, should directors wish to do so, they may choose to have the Socrates of the later two acts seated in the theatre during act 1. Ambitious directors may even encourage the audience to take note of this fact since, according to Aelian, when the Socrates character appeared onstage and began to be referred to, a number of foreigners who were in attendance who had never seen Socrates

> began to murmur and ask who this man Socrates was. When he heard this – he was in fact present, not as a result of luck or chance, but because he knew that he was the subject of the play, and he sat in a prominent position in the theatre – at any rate, in order to put an end to the foreigners' ignorance, he stood up and remained standing in full view throughout the play as the actors performed it.[4]

If the decision is made to have Socrates observe the first act in this way, a short explanatory comment may need to be added to the introductory remarks at the beginning of act 1.

In act 1 and act 3 the same actors should represent the Stronger and Weaker Arguments, although in act 3 it needs to be made clear that both Arguments are now prepared to discuss much more serious topics than in act 1. The same actor should portray Crito in act 2 and act 3. In act 2, both Crito and Plato are to be seated in the house near the back. Minor speaking and non-speaking roles – such as those of Callias, the Politicians, the Poets, the Craftsmen, the Juryman, Thetis, Achilles, and the Hecklers – can easily be assigned to members of the Chorus, especially if the decision is made to keep the Chorus onstage as observers during this act.

The introductory remarks at the beginning of each act will normally be made by the Leader of the Chorus, although other options are also possible, such as having a separate Narrator or a different member of the cast introduce each act. At the director's discretion, these comments may also be shortened or even eliminated. Although the second act is set outdoors at the Athenian Areopagus rather than in a courtroom or courtyard, nothing significant hinges on this setting.

This script grew out of a shorter dramatic reading of the same name based on Steve Wexler's translation of the *Apology* and performed at the University of British Columbia in February 2006 with Joan Bryans, director, Andrew Irvine, producer, and Steve Wexler in the role of Socrates. The first production involving a modified version of the current script was presented in March 2007 at the University of British Columbia Chan Centre for the Performing Arts. The premiere involved the following artistic team:

| | |
|---|---|
| *Narrator* | Ian Brooks |
| *Townsfolk* | Odessa Cadieux-Rey, John Harris, Daryl Hutchings, Laura McLean, Mark McPherran, Bill Wu |
| *Pheidippides* | Mark Penney |
| *Strepsiades* | John Burnside |
| *Student 1* | Zoe Green-Riley |
| *Student 2* | Steve Baumber |
| *1st Chorus* | Ian Brooks, Julie Cohn, Miranda Duffy, Hailey McCarthy-Goode, Kevin Sloan |
| *Students* | Odessa Cadieux-Rey, Shaun Kaser, Laura McLean, Mercury Rhone, Anika Vervecken |

| | |
|---|---|
| *Socrates (in middle age)* | Crispin Bryce |
| *Sun* | Shaun Kaser |
| *Moon* | Odessa Cadieux-Rey |
| *Stronger Argument* | Daryl Hutchings |
| *Weaker Argument* | Steve Baumber |
| *2nd Chorus* | Steve Baumber, Ian Brooks, Julie Cohn, Hailey McCarthy-Goode, Laura McLean |
| *Drummer* | Miranda Duffy |
| *Archon* | Mark McPherran |
| *Lykon* | John Harris |
| *Anytus* | Daryl Hutchings |
| *Meletus* | Mercury Rhone |
| *Guards* | Odessa Cadieux-Rey, Bill Wu |
| *Socrates (in old age)* | Steve Wexler |
| *Hecklers* | Zoe Green-Riley, Shaun Kaser, Mark Penney, Kevin Sloan, Anika Vervecken |
| *Achilles* | Steve Baumber |
| *Thetis* | Miranda Duffy |
| *Crito* | Shaun Kaser |
| *Plato* | Mark Penney |
| | |
| *Producer* | Andrew Irvine |
| *Director* | Joan Bryans |
| *Composer* | Michael Rummen |
| *Set Designer* | John R. Taylor |
| *Lighting Designer* | Mimi Abrahams |
| *Costume Designer* | Catherine E. Carr |
| *Sound Designer* | Darren W. Hales |
| *Stage Manager* | Laura Moore |
| *Assistant Director / Rehearsal Stage Manager* | Frances Herzer |
| *Assistant Stage Manager* | Sarah Banting |
| *Graphic Designer* | Sandi McDonald |
| *Photographers* | Martin Dee, Doug Williams |
| *Production Assistants* | Johnna Fisher, Nissa Wainwright |
| *Production Crew* | Debbi Abrami, Steve Baumber, Sunny Chen, Laura Jones, Ted Shear, Jihyun Yun |

# Classroom Notes

The current script has been written not only for onstage performance, but also for use in the classroom. It is hoped that college and university instructors especially will find the script flexible enough to be used in a variety of in-class contexts.

Although the play is normally intended to include all three acts, both the first and second acts may be used as the basis for shorter, stand-alone plays. Act 1 has a running time of approximately forty minutes, act 2 a running time of approximately sixty minutes, and act 3 a running time of approximately twenty minutes. The exact time to complete the vote in act 2 will depend on the size of the jury. Should the production need to be shortened, it is easy to do so by eliminating some of the dialogue in act 2.

Instructors with large classes may assign one or more acts as optional projects for groups of student volunteers, perhaps in place of a midterm essay or exam. Instructors with smaller classes may want to involve the entire class. Performances may be held in front of the class itself or in front of invited audiences.

For instructors not wanting to mount elaborate theatrical productions, all three acts may also be used as the basis for in-class dramatic readings. Even simply having students read the play aloud in class is often enough to encourage a more detailed reading of the original texts. The fact that the current script diverges from these texts in important ways can also serve as an incentive for debate. Given the significant demands of memorization placed on the Socrates character in act 2, a polished dramatic reading of this act (for example, with Socrates standing behind a podium rather than on an open stage) may be appropriate even in more traditional theatrical venues.

In more elaborate contexts, the script may again be used in a variety of ways. For example, during the first act masks may be worn. If worn, they will add to the play's authenticity and remind audiences that they are watching a fictional story being performed much as it was 2,400 years ago.[1] Even so, especially when working with beginning performers, masks are often best avoided. Not only do they add significantly to preparation and rehearsal times, they also make much greater demands on the abilities of both actors and directors. Masks should not be worn during act 2 or act 3, since both acts are meant to recount genuine historical episodes rather than ancient theatrical performances.

Dress may be either classical or modern, although if classical dress is worn, students may need to be reminded that during this period Greek men wore tunics, sometimes together with a cloak, not Roman togas.[2] According to legend, Socrates went barefoot most of his life.

In act 2, the Archon should not be confused with a modern judge. Instead, he functioned more like a court clerk and would have ensured that the trial began on time, that speeches were properly timed with a water clock, and that no one tampered with the jury. In Socrates' day, the jury itself dealt with matters of law now normally dealt with by a judge.[3]

Sets and lighting may be minimal or more elaborate but, in general, the less elaborate the better. Set transitions need to be accomplished with a minimum of fuss and bother and are often best done without blackouts. In all respects, the play works just as well in a theatre-in-the-round as it does on a traditional stage.

During the initial act, when the Socrates character is first seen with his head in the clouds, the set may be designed so that he is simply standing at a high point on the stage. In more elaborate settings, a crane (controlling either a basket or a trapeze) may be used to hold Socrates among the clouds and then lower him to the ground, just as was originally done at the ancient Theatre of Dionysus. To indicate the passage of time, directors may wish to have actors playing the part of the Sun and the Moon pass near the front of the stage. Alternatively, mechanical equivalents may be used as part of a more elaborate set but, once again, less elaborate accompaniments often work the best.

In the first act, the main requirement for a successful Chorus is sufficient rehearsal to keep the pace quick and diction clear. Typically, the smaller the Chorus, the fewer the rehearsals required to produce a sufficiently high degree of coordination among Chorus members. Instead of being recited in unison as in a choir, most lines or stanzas should be alternated between individual Chorus members. Although Aristophanes' original play required the Chorus to be composed of clouds, there is no such requirement in the current script. Directors are free to reintroduce this feature should they want to do so.

The size of the Chorus, the size of the jury, and the number of players in minor roles (Students, Hecklers, Guards, Friends, etc.) may easily be varied to suit the local context. Experience has shown that faculty members as well as students enjoy being invited to play minor as well as major roles.

Depending on local audience expectations, some warning concerning profanity – or at least earthy vulgarity – may be desirable.

# Pronunciation of Greek Names

The correct pronunciation of ancient Greek names, like the correct pronunciation of ancient Greek words more generally, has been a topic of debate since at least the time of Erasmus in the sixteenth century.[1] Today, matters are complicated by the fact that over the centuries several distinct traditions governing the pronunciation of classical names have arisen. Even so, anglicized pronunciations (for example, the use of *Playt′ oh*, rather than *Plat′ on* when referring to Socrates' most famous pupil) remain acceptable in most contexts. The phonetic versions of the names listed below respect this convention and give the most common contemporary English pronunciations.[2]

Syllables receiving primary stress are followed by an accent (′). Long vowels are written as follows: 'ay' for *a*, 'ee' for *e*, 'y' for *i*, 'oh' for *o*, and 'yoo' for *u*. 'Th' is pronounced throughout as in *think* or *thank*, not as in *this* or *that*. A hard *g* (as in *Greek*) is represented by *g*; a soft *g* (as in *gesture*) is represented by *j*. A hard *c* (as in *can*) is represented by *k*; a soft *c* (as in *census*) is represented by *s*. Other consonants are pronounced as in English.

Achilles (a kil′ eez)
Acropolis (a krop′ o lis)
Adeimantos (a day mant′ us)
Aeantodorus (ee an to dor′ us)
Aelian (eel′ i an)
Aeschines (ee′ skin eez)
Agora (a′ gor a)
Aiacus (y′ a kos *or* ee′ a kus)
Alcibiades (al si by′ a deez *or* al ki by′ a deez)

Alexamenos of Teos (a lex′ a men os *of* tee′ os)
Amphipolis (am phip′ o lis)
Anaxagoras (an ax ag′ or as)
Antiphon the Kephisian (an′ ti fon *the* kef is′ i an)
Anytus (an y′ tus)
Apollo (a pol′ oh)
Apollodorus (a pol o doh′ rus)
Areopagus (a re o′ pa gus)

Arginusae (arg in y oo´ see *or*
  arg in oo´ see)
Ariston (ar ist´ ohn)
Aristophanes (ar is to´ fan eez)
Aristotle (ar´ is to tul)
Asclepius (ask lee´ pius)
Athena (ath ee´ na)
Athens (ath´ ens)
Attica (a´ tic a)

Basileios (bas´ il ee os)

Callias (kal´ i as)
Chaerephon (ky´ re fon)
Charmides (karm´ i deez)
Cicero (sis´ er oh)
Cratylus (krat´ i lus)
Critias (krit´ i as)
Crito (kry´ toh)
Critobulus (kry to bu´ lus *or*
  kry to´ bu lus)
Croesus of Lydia (kree´ sus *of*
  lid´ ee a)

Delium (deel´ i um)
Delos (dee´ los)
Delphi (del´ fee)
Diodorus Siculus (dy oh´ dohr us
  sic yoo´ lus)
Diogenes Laertius (dy o´ jen eez
  lay ur´ shus)
Dionysia (dy on ys´ i a)
Dionysus (dy on ys´ us)

Ephialtes (ef i al´ teez)
Epigenes (e pi´ jen eez)
Euthyphro (yoo´ thi froh)
Evenus of Paros (ev een´ us *of*
  par´ os)

Gorgias of Leontini (gohr´ ji as *or*
  gohrg´ i as *of* lee ont´ i nee)

Hades (hay´ deez)
Hector (hek´ tor)
Heliaia (heel ee y´ a)
Hermogenes (herm´ o jen eez)
Herodotus (her od´ o tus)
Hesiod (hees´ i od *or* hes´ i od)
Hippias of Elis (hip´ ee as *of*
  ee´ lis)
Hipponicus (hi pon´ i kus)
Homer (hohm´ er)

Lamprokles (lamp´ roh kleez)
Leon of Salamis (lee´ on *of*
  sal´ a mis)
Lykon (ly´ kon)
Lysanias the Sphettian (lis ayn´ i
  as *the* sfet´ ee an)

Marathon (ma´ ra thon)
Meletus (mel eet´ us)
Menexenos (men´ ex e nos)
Minos (min´ os *or* myn´ os)
Myrto (mert´ oh)

Nicostratus (nik os trat´ us *or*
  nik os trayt´ us)

Odysseus (od is´ y oos *or*
  od is´ ee us)
Orpheus (orf´ y oos *or* orf´ ee us)
Otanes (o ta´ neez)

Parnassus (par nas´ us)
Parthenon (par´ then on)
Patroclus (pa trok´ lus)
Peloponnese (pel oh pon ees´)

Pericles (pe´ ri kleez)
Phaedo (fee´ doh)
Phaedrus (fee´ drus)
Pheidippides (fy dip´ i deez)
Pheidon (fy´ dohn)
Plato (playt´ oh)
Plutarch (ploot´ ark)
Pnyx (pnix)
Potidaea (pot i dee´ a)
Prodikos of Ceos (proh´ di kos or
    pro´ di kos of kee´ os)
Protagoras (proh tag´ or as)
Prytaneum (prit a nee´ um)

Rhadamanthus (rad am anth´ us)

Simon (sy´ mon)
Sisyphus (sis´ i fus)
Socrates (so´ kra teez)
Sophroniskos (sof´ ron is kos)

Sparta (spar´ ta)
Stoa (stoh´ a)
Strepsiades (strep sy´ a deez)

Theaetetus (thee y tet´ us or
    thee a teet´ us)
Theodotus (theo´ do tus)
Theozotides (thee oh zot´ i deez)
Theseus (thee´ see us)
Thessaly (thess´ a lee)
Thetis (thee´ tis)
Thucydides (thoo syd´ i deez)
Triptolemus (trip tol´ e mus)
Troy (troi)

Xanthippe (zan thip´ ee)
Xenophon (zen´ o fon)

Zeus (zyoos or zoos)

# Socrates on Trial

# List of Characters

(in order of appearance)

**Act 1:** *Clouds* (in ancient Athens)

*Leader of the Chorus*
*Strepsiades* (an Athenian businessman)
*Chorus* (perhaps half a dozen, or fewer)
*Student 1* (a member of the School of Thinkology)
*Student 2* (a member of the School of Thinkology)
*Students* (non-speaking, perhaps half a dozen)
*Socrates* (Greece's most famous philosopher, in middle age)
*Sun* (non-speaking)
*Moon* (non-speaking)
*Pheidippides* (the son of Strepsiades)
*Stronger Argument* (personified in age)
*Weaker Argument* (personified in youth)

**Act 2:** *Apology* (twenty-four years later)

*Leader of the Chorus*
*Archon* (an Athenian magistrate)
*Dignitaries* (non-speaking, perhaps two or three)
*Meletus* (Socrates' chief accuser)
*Anytus* (Socrates' second accuser)
*Lykon* (Socrates' third accuser)
*Guard* (non-speaking)
*Socrates* (Greece's most famous philosopher, in vigorous old age)
*Hecklers* (perhaps half a dozen, or more)

*Callias* (a father from Paros)
*Politicians* (non-speaking)
*Poets* (non-speaking)
*Craftsmen* (non-speaking)
*Juryman* (an ordinary Athenian citizen)
*Thetis* (the mother of Achilles)
*Achilles* (Greece's greatest warrior)
*Plato* (Socrates' student)
*Crito* (Socrates' best friend)

## Act 3: *Crito* and *Phaedo* (one month later)

*Leader of the Chorus*
*Socrates* (Greece's most famous philosopher, in vigorous old age)
*Crito* (Socrates' best friend)
*Stronger Argument* (personified in age)
*Weaker Argument* (personified in youth)
*Xanthippe* (Socrates' wife)
*Friends* (non-speaking, both men and women, as many as a dozen or
    more)
*Executioner* (strong enough to wrestle unwilling prisoners)
*Chorus* (either in whole or in part)

# Act One
## *Clouds*

Welcome everyone. I want to thank you for joining us.

During Greece's Golden Age, rather than staying home to be taught by their parents, many young men had begun studying under itinerant teachers called *sophists*. It was this perversion of the natural order that led Aristophanes to write the *Clouds* – a play that's part slapstick comedy, part vulgar gossip, and part bawdy vaudeville show. In fact, some of Aristophanes' dialogue is almost guaranteed to make you blush!

Aristophanes' play tells the story of how a father named Strepsiades takes his lazy, longhaired son – Pheidippides – to be taught by one of Athens' new intellectuals.

The teacher Strepsiades visits is named Socrates, although the *real* Socrates will want to warn you that the Socrates you see onstage is nothing more than a comic distortion invented by Aristophanes for the sake of a few cheap laughs.

We get to hear from the real Socrates after the intermission when we return for a presentation of Plato's famous *Apology*. This is Plato's dramatization of the speech Socrates gave in his own defence after he'd been charged with corrupting the young and failing to recognize the traditional Greek gods.

The jury in front of which Socrates spoke was large, perhaps five hundred or more of his fellow citizens. This made it more difficult for jury members

(*while offering a member of the audience a bribe*)

to be bribed.

*(while withdrawing the bribe as the audience member reaches out)*
Too slow!

In today's performance, everyone here will be serving as jurors.[†]
After Socrates' speech, you'll be asked to cast your vote in favour
of his guilt or innocence.

But before we get to Socrates' trial, we first get to enjoy Aristophanes' play, and learn why Strepsiades feels that, rather than
being educated, his son has been corrupted by the new-fangled
educators of his day.

We join Strepsiades just as he's about to knock on the door of a
peculiar little building on the edge of Athens called the 'School of
Thinkology.'

THE SCHOOL OF THINKOLOGY *on the edge of Athens. Day. Onstage, a father,*
STREPSIADES, *is about to knock on a door. Above the door is a sign saying*
*'School of Thinkology.'* STREPSIADES *knocks. There's no answer. He knocks*
*again.*

STREPSIADES

*(to the audience)*
Why won't they answer? That useless, good-for-nothing son of
mine has accumulated so many gambling debts. Now his creditors
are banging at my door. And I can't think of anything to do about
it except this.

STREPSIADES *knocks again.*

STREPSIADES *(cont'd)*

*(to the audience)*
Some days, I wish that damn matchmaker had never even hooked
me up with his mother. I was having a lovely time 'til then, lying
around, eating honey and olives, doing as I pleased. Then I got
married!
*(fondly)*
I still remember. She was from the city and smelled of perfume. We
had long kisses. And lots of sex ...

---

[†] This sentence may need to be modified depending upon the size of the audience.

(*building in emphasis to ensure that everyone is impressed*)
Lots of sex! ... Lots of sex!
(*more realistically*)
But the responsibility! I won't say she's lazy, but neither she nor
our son appreciates how hard it is to make ends meet. Just spend,
spend, spend. Especially our boy, Pheidippides. And it's because
of *his* gambling that the creditors want to confiscate *my* stuff.

STREPSIADES *knocks again.*

STREPSIADES (*cont'd*)
(*to the audience, indicating the School of Thinkology*)
These so-called wisdom lovers. From what I hear, they really love
only themselves and their money. But they do know how to twist
an argument, I'll give 'em that. Experts in rhetorical chicanery,
that's what they are. And for a few coins, I'm told they can teach
me how to turn even the weakest argument into a winning one. If
anyone can help me escape my boy's debts, they can.

As STREPSIADES *continues to knock, the* CHORUS *performs.*

CHORUS
Now here's a man who seeks to be wise,
But who lacks good judgement, whatever he tries.
With training and work, he hopes he'll succeed
At mastering the skills he thinks his soul needs.

He'll study and learn, with no fear of the cold,
He's sure he can't fail, even though he's quite old.
With a sharp, focused mind, using skills he deplores,
He knows victory's assured in his legal wars.

STREPSIADES
(*loudly*)
Is anyone home?

*A hatch in the door opens suddenly.* STUDENT 1 *appears.*

STUDENT 1
Go to hell!

*The hatch slams shut.*

#### STREPSIADES
(*shaking his coin purse*)
But how can I pay you for your wisdom if you won't open the door?

*The hatch reopens.* STUDENT 1 *and* STUDENT 2 *appear.*

#### STUDENT 1
Who are you?

#### STREPSIADES
Strepsiades, son of Pheidon, father of Pheidippides.

#### STUDENT 2
You *should* be called *Stupidities*! Banging away like that. Don't you know we're busy *thinking* in here?

#### STREPSIADES
Oh, I'm sorry. But I want to become a student. You see, it's almost the end of the month, and interest will be due soon.

#### STUDENT 2
You're not making any sense.

#### STUDENT 1
But did you bring your tuition?

#### STREPSIADES
(*showing his coin purse*)
I did.

*The door opens and out steps* STUDENT 1 *from within the School of Thinkology.*

#### STUDENT 1
Then perhaps we could have a short talk.

*Out steps* STUDENT 2 *from within the School of Thinkology.*

STREPSIADES

This is Socrates' school, isn't it? I don't want to disturb the great man, but I really must speak with him. Is he deep in thought?

STUDENT 1

He is.

STREPSIADES

Tell me! What about?

STUDENT 2

He's considering an important scientific matter.

STREPSIADES

What?

STUDENT 1

Whether the buzzing of a gnat is made through its mouth, or its anus.

STREPSIADES

Tell me! What's he concluded?

STUDENT 1

(*pompously*)
He's concluded that a gnat's intestine is narrow –

STUDENT 2

(*interrupting*)
Extremely constricted –

STUDENT 1

(*interrupting*)
And it's because of this constriction that air is pushed with great force through a small orifice –

STUDENT 2

(*interrupting*)
Towards its rear –

STUDENT 1
(*interrupting*)
Resulting in the transmission of vibrations –

STUDENT 2
(*interrupting*)
And other not disagreeable sounds –

STUDENT 1
(*interrupting*)
Caused by the outward rushing of air.

*Out steps a group of additional* STUDENTS *from within the School of Think-ology.* STUDENT 2 *ushers them aside and begins placing them in peculiar posi-tions. Once in position, they are all bending over, looking at the ground.*

STREPSIADES
(*to* STUDENT 1)
So a gnat's ass is really a trumpet! Brilliant! What a genius he must be.
(*to the audience, laughing*)
And with such a deep understanding of assholes, I bet he's an expert in fending off lawyers!

STUDENT 1 *rolls his eyes.* STREPSIADES *notices the additional* STUDENTS. STUDENT 2 *is coaxing them to stay in position.*

STUDENT 2
Concentrate. Concentrate.
(*adjusting a* STUDENT'S *position*)
That's better.

STREPSIADES
Are these his students?

STUDENT 1
They are.

STREPSIADES
Why are they looking at the ground like that?

STUDENT 2

They're searching for important discoveries beneath the surface of
the earth.

STREPSIADES

And why are their butts pointing towards the heavens?

STUDENT 2

Directed studies in '*ass*-tronomy!'

STUDENT 1

He's coming!

STUDENT 2
(*to the* STUDENTS, *clapping his hands*)
Inside! Quickly, quickly!

*The* STUDENTS *begin entering the School of Thinkology.*

STREPSIADES

Wait a minute! Can't they stay a little longer?

STREPSIADES *exposes his leather phallus and begins stroking it; or, if in modern dress, he makes a rude hand gesture.*

STREPSIADES (*cont'd*)

I've a point or two I'd like to share with them.

STUDENT 1

You can't.

STUDENT 2

It's not allowed.

STUDENT 1

At least not now.

SOCRATES *appears high above the stage with his head in the clouds.*

CHORUS

High above the clouds
The unwearied eye of heaven,
Blazes forth with glittering beams.

Here we see the peak of man,
Destroyer of the gods!
Reason incarnate, the fulfilment of our dreams.

Shake off this misty shapelessness
From your immortal form,
For wisdom personified is never as it seems.

STUDENT 2

Here's the man you're looking for.

STREPSIADES

Who?

STUDENT 1

Socrates. Up there, with his head in the clouds.

STREPSIADES

What's he doing?

STUDENT 2

He's investigating important celestial phenomena.

STREPSIADES

Why not do it down here on the ground?

STUDENT 2

If he did, he'd never come up with any *elevated* ideas. It's only by
being up there, among the clouds, that he's able to turn his mind to
*lofty* thoughts.

STREPSIADES

By Zeus! He's high enough to see the gods!

STUDENT 1

Socrates has discovered there are no gods.

STREPSIADES

No gods? Then who brings the rain?

STUDENT 2

Rain comes from clouds, not gods.

STREPSIADES

I always thought it came from Zeus.

STUDENT 1

If it was Zeus, he should be able to make it rain even when the sky's clear. But have you ever seen it rain without clouds?

STREPSIADES

By Apollo, that's a good point. I'd always thought it was Zeus pissing through a sieve. And when he farted, that was thunder.

*The* STUDENTS *roll their eyes.*

STREPSIADES (*cont'd*)

Now I'm even more convinced I need to speak with him. Can you ask him to come down?

STUDENT 1

(*while* STUDENT 1 *and* STUDENT 2 *converse with another* STUDENT *through the hatch in the school door*)

You'll have to do it yourself. We're too busy.

STREPSIADES

Socrates! Socrates! Can you hear me?

STUDENT 2

You'll have to call louder than that.

STREPSIADES

Socrates! Is that you?

SOCRATES

(*looking around*)
Whose voice do I hear?

STREPSIADES

Oh, Socrates, I need you to come down!

SOCRATES

It's a small, insignificant voice –

STREPSIADES

(*interrupting*)
Please! I need to talk to you.

SOCRATES

The voice of an insect, or a bug –

STREPSIADES

(*interrupting*)
I'm willing to pay you. I need you to teach me your wisdom.

SOCRATES

(*finally noticing* STREPSIADES)
And why is that?

*As* STREPSIADES *speaks,* SOCRATES *begins his descent.*

STREPSIADES

I need to learn how to argue. The creditors and bailiffs are banging at my door!

SOCRATES

(*finding the descent difficult*)
Ooof!

STREPSIADES

They're slapping liens on all my property. Unless you can help me, I won't have anything left. Then what good will I be to myself? Or my family?

SOCRATES
(*falling face down onto the ground*)
Arrrhg.


STREPSIADES
Only a truly great man – like you – can save me from ruin.


SOCRATES *stands up and dusts himself off.*


SOCRATES
So how did you come to amass such enormous debts?


STREPSIADES
Oh, I tried to keep my extravagant son in check. But he's too much for me. Between his gambling, and maintaining his horses and chariots, he spends more money than I can earn.


SOCRATES
I see.


STREPSIADES
So I need you to teach me your hair-splitting arguments. You know, the way you turn a weaker argument into a stronger one. So I can go to court and win even an unjust cause. Name your price, whatever it takes. I promise by all the gods, I'll pay you!


SOCRATES
(*laughing*)
'Promise by all the gods'? We don't extend credit to the gods here!


STUDENT 1 *holds out his hand.*


STUDENT 1
Payment in advance, please.


STUDENT 2
You could hardly hope to have the great Socrates teach you how to avoid paying your tuition, now could you?

STREPSIADES

Of course! I mean, of course not. I mean ... I mean I don't trust the
gods either. If I ran into them, I'd refuse to speak to them. And you
won't catch me making sacrifices, or pouring libations to them,
either. No sir. Not at all.

*As* STREPSIADES *begins counting out his coins, the* CHORUS *performs.*

CHORUS

Now here's a man who's a slippery fraud,
He'll go without food and abandon the gods.
In public he says he's courageous and bold,
But in private he'll do whatever he's told.

He'll lie and he'll cheat to avoid paying his debts,
And anything else to protect his assets.
He'll master his logic, he'll learn to split hairs,
And soon all who meet him will have to take care.

STREPSIADES *finishes counting out his coins.* STUDENT 1 *and* STUDENT 2 *take
the coins and exit into the School of Thinkology.*

SOCRATES

So tell me, what sort of man are you? If we're going to develop a
winning strategy, I'll need to know more about you.

STREPSIADES

A 'winning strategy'? You sound like a military man. Are you
going to assault me?

SOCRATES

No, no. I just need you to tell me about yourself. Do you have a
good memory?

STREPSIADES

Well, it varies. If someone owes me money, my memory's terrific.
But if I owe them money, it's not so good.

SOCRATES

Do you have a natural gift for persuasive speech?

STREPSIADES

(*laughing*)
I try to persuade people that I don't need to pay my debts, if that's
what you mean.

SOCRATES
Aren't you interested in *anything* except money?

STREPSIADES
Of course! I'm also interested in meeting people who *have* money.
    (*noticing* SOCRATES' *poor clothes*)
I don't suppose you know anyone like that, do you?

SOCRATES
Look, unless you focus on what's important, how can I teach you
anything?

STREPSIADES
Don't worry, mate. I'll catch on. You'll see.

CHORUS
Grasping subtle belief and lofty thought
Requires concentration, a mind that's taut.
So lift high your thoughts, up to the sky
Where wisdom floats and concepts lie.

If you try your best, you won't go wrong
And among philosophers you'll soon belong.
The days will pass, and the night time too,
But when all is done, your lessons you'll rue.

SOCRATES
Then let's get to work.

*As the* SUN *and* MOON *rotate by, the* CHORUS *indicates the passing of several
days.*

CHORUS
Day.
Followed by night.

Followed by day.
Followed by night.
Followed by day.

*THE SCHOOL OF THINKOLOGY on the edge of Athens. Several days later.* SOCRATES *is facing the audience.* STREPSIADES *is distracted and not paying attention.*

SOCRATES
(*to the audience*)
By all the gods! I've never met anyone so crude, stupid, clumsy, and forgetful. He tries to learn the tiniest things, and then forgets them before he's even half done.
(*to* STREPSIADES)
Now, Strepsiades, old man, let's try again. Look over here.
(*using a stick to point to a map drawn on the ground*)
Here's a map of the world. See? Right there. That's Athens.

STREPSIADES
(*looking at the ground*)
What do you mean? I don't see the Parthenon. Or any jurymen sitting on their benches.

SOCRATES
And here's Attica.

STREPSIADES
Then where's my house? And where's Sparta?

SOCRATES
Here.

STREPSIADES
Oh no it's not. Look how close it is to Athens. Sparta's five days' march from here. You'd better move it if you want anyone to believe you.

SOCRATES
Move it?

STREPSIADES

Yes, by all the gods. And if you care for Athens' safety, you'll move it far away.

(*threateningly*)

Do it now. Or I'll make you cry!


SOCRATES

(*in exasperation*)

Look, you've got to concentrate. Of all the things you've never learned, what do you want to study most? Formal diction? Rhythmic verse? Musical scales? Measures?


STREPSIADES

Measures! Just last week that bastard who sells barley in the marketplace cheated me out of two full measures on his scales!


SOCRATES

Not that kind of measure! Have you never heard of a *musical* scale? If a poem were set to music, which measure would be more beautiful? A three-quarter beat?

SOCRATES *begins beating a rhythm with his fist against his hand.*


SOCRATES (*cont'd*)

One, two, three. One, two, three. One, two, three. Or a four-quarter beat?

SOCRATES *changes the rhythm.*


SOCRATES (*cont'd*)

One, two, three, four. One, two, three, four.


STREPSIADES

Finally, something I know! I've known how to beat with my hand since I was a boy!


SOCRATES

You have? Show me.

STREPSIADES *exposes his leather phallus and begins rubbing it; or, if in modern dress, he makes a rude hand gesture.*

SOCRATES (*cont'd*)

By the gods! I've never seen such a vulgar man. You're nothing but a fool!

STREPSIADES

You're the fool!

SOCRATES

I bet you don't even know your sums. Do you know what a number is? Or a digit?

STREPSIADES

(*angrily*)
Everyone knows what a digit is!

SOCRATES

Show me.

STREPSIADES *rudely sticks his middle finger straight up.* SOCRATES *is taken aback.*

STREPSIADES

I didn't come here to learn any of this fancy stuff.

SOCRATES

Well, what did you come to learn?

STREPSIADES

You know. The *other* thing. Because my debts are weighing me down ... my son ... his horses ... remember? I need my bankers to think I'm a real legal eagle. *Sly!* I need you to teach me that secret thing. You know:
   (*whispering*)
How to make the weaker argument appear to be the stronger!

SOCRATES

That's an advanced class.

STREPSIADES

Please!

SOCRATES

Well, perhaps for a slightly higher fee.

STUDENT 1 *reappears from nowhere with his hand outstretched. As* STREPSIA-DES *counts out several coins, the* CHORUS *performs.*

CHORUS

Now ponder and think, focus this way and that.
Let your mind float. Avoid the claptrap.
Be bold and be glib, be sharp and be wise,
Think deep, deep thoughts. And analyze!

When you can't sleep, as you mind turns and tosses,
Focus on logic, and not on your losses.
Quickly old man, for your family's sake,
Learn from your master. Your mind educate!

STUDENT 1 *exits.*

SOCRATES

Now here's something to think about. What would you do if you were being sued, let's say for five talents? How would you win your case?

STREPSIADES

Five talents? That's a lot of money.

SOCRATES

Start by carving your slender thoughts into tiny bits, and then think the matter through. Let your mind float freely, up, into the clouds.

STREPSIADES

Okay. Okay. Oh, this is brilliant!

SOCRATES

I'm listening.

STREPSIADES

You'll like this. What if I hired a Thessalian witch? Then, when night comes, she could haul down the moon and lock it in a box.

SOCRATES

How would that help?

STREPSIADES

Don't you see? If the moon never rose, I wouldn't have to pay anyone! They only charge interest at the start of each new moon!

SOCRATES

(*rolling his eyes*)
You'll have to do better than that.

STREPSIADES

Okay. Okay. Oh, I've got it. This is *so* good.

SOCRATES

I'm listening.

STREPSIADES

At the shop where the healers sell the drugs, have you seen those pretty stones? You know, the ones you can see straight through. That they use to start fires.

SOCRATES

You mean ... glass?

STREPSIADES

That's the stuff! What if I stole some glass? Then, when the court clerk was writing out the charge, I'd stand between him and the sun – like this – some distance off. I'd make the writing on his wax tablet melt! At least the part about me!

SOCRATES

Oh sweet mercy!

STREPSIADES

It is sweet. I'd erase a five-talent lawsuit!

SOCRATES

Let's try once more.

STREPSIADES

I'm ready.

SOCRATES

You've been charged in court. The evidence has been presented and you're about to lose. How would you avoid the charge, even without a witness?

STREPSIADES

No problem.

SOCRATES

I'm listening.

STREPSIADES

I'd run home and hang myself!

SOCRATES *rubs his sore head.*

STREPSIADES (*cont'd*)

Don't you see? It's a terrific idea! How can anyone sue me if I'm dead?

SOCRATES

You're talking rubbish! Go home! I'm not going to spend another minute with you.

SOCRATES *re-enters his school.*

STREPSIADES

Oh no! I've been expelled!
    Chorus, this is terrible! I should have known I was too old to learn this new skill of tongue twisting. Without being able to twist words and split hairs, how can I avoid my creditors?

CHORUS

You see, old man, at your fine age,
You find it hard to act the sage.

But you've a son who's fully grown,
Why not take him, his skills to hone?

STREPSIADES

Of course! But he's too busy with his horses. He won't want to
learn this stuff any more than I do.

CHORUS

He wants one thing,
You another.
But who's his father?
You? Or his mother?

STREPSIADES

You're right, Chorus. Of course you're right. I know what I have to
do.

STREPSIADES *exits. As the* SUN *and* MOON *rotate by, the* CHORUS *indicates
the passing of several days.*

CHORUS

Day.
Followed by night.
Followed by day.
Followed by night.
Followed by day.

*THE* SCHOOL OF THINKOLOGY *on the edge of Athens. Several days later.*
STREPSIADES *enters with his son* PHEIDIPPIDES.

PHEIDIPPIDES

You're being unreasonable. This time my horse can't lose!

STREPSIADES

That's what you said last time. *And* the time before that.

PHEIDIPPIDES

But can't you see? I'm just one win away from erasing my debts.
Zeus himself will be on my side this time!

STREPSIADES

Zeus? You can't believe in Zeus at your age. There is no Zeus. It's
time you grew up.
(*indicating the School of Thinkology*)
It's time you went to school!


PHEIDIPPIDES

School? With that cult of wisdom-lovers? Never! There's nothing
even remotely useful I could learn in there.


STREPSIADES

Nothing useful? What about measures you can hear? Or scales that
don't weigh? What about magic glass? What about learning how
thick and stupid you are!


PHEIDIPPIDES

(*to the audience*)
My father's lost his wits. What should I do? Perhaps I should take
him to court and get him committed.

STREPSIADES *knocks on the School door.*


STREPSIADES

(*sweetly*)
Socrates! Oh Socrates!

*There is no answer.*


PHEIDIPPIDES

(*to the audience, jokingly*)
Maybe I should take him straight to the coffin-maker!

STREPSIADES *kicks the School door.*


STREPSIADES

(*angrily*)
Socrates, if you don't open the door I'll call the authorities!


PHEIDIPPIDES

(*to the audience, slightly intimidated*)
Perhaps it's safest if I just play along.

*The door opens and* SOCRATES *appears.*

SOCRATES

Strepsiades!

STREPSIADES

Oh, Socrates! I'm too old to learn all the wisdom you have to teach
me. So I've brought my son instead.

SOCRATES

Your son?

STREPSIADES

He'll learn, you'll see. He's gifted. When he was little – just this tall
– even then you should have seen him. He built little houses. And
made little boats out of old shoes. Get him to learn those two arguments. You know. The stronger one, whatever that is. And the
*weaker* one – the one that lets you argue an unjust cause and win. If
you don't have time to teach him both, then at least teach him the
tricky one.

STUDENT 1 *reappears from nowhere with his hand outstretched. As* STREPSIA-
DES *begins counting out his coins, the* CHORUS *performs.*

CHORUS

You'll get what you want –
   Careful –
What you think you desire –
   Careful –
But be careful, old man –
   Careful –
Things sometimes backfire!

*Before he finishes counting out his coins,* STREPSIADES *just hands over his
entire purse.* STUDENT 1 *takes the purse and exits.*

SOCRATES

(*to* STREPSIADES, *looking* PHEIDIPPIDES *over*)
All right. But first, tell me: what's it like to be in business?

STREPSIADES
In business, it's screw or be screwed.

SOCRATES
I see. And which do you prefer?

STREPSIADES
Well, that's the whole point, isn't it? I'd rather not get screwed. The problem is how to avoid it.

SOCRATES
But you've avoided it so far, have you?

STREPSIADES
Well, yes. But just barely.

SOCRATES
So if others haven't been so lucky, you'll clearly be in the advantageous position, even if you think you're not.

STREPSIADES
I suppose.

SOCRATES
Then let's see how easy it will be for your son to learn what he needs to know. He can learn it from the Arguments themselves. First, there's the Stronger Argument.

*The* STRONGER ARGUMENT *enters, personified by age.*

SOCRATES (*cont'd*)
Then, there's the Weaker Argument.

STRONGER ARGUMENT
  (*to the offstage* WEAKER ARGUMENT)
Come on. Come on.
  (*to the audience, referring to the* WEAKER ARGUMENT)
Slow and lazy, as always.

*The* WEAKER ARGUMENT *enters, personified by youth.*

WEAKER ARGUMENT
(*to the* STRONGER ARGUMENT, *but looking at the audience*)
Wow! Have you seen this crowd? I'm going to enjoy demolishing
you this time!

STRONGER ARGUMENT
You? Demolish me? Who do you think you are?

WEAKER ARGUMENT
(*with cheeky confidence*)
Just an argument.

STRONGER ARGUMENT
(*condescendingly*)
A *weaker* argument.

WEAKER ARGUMENT
Ohhh, aren't you the superior one. I may be weaker, darling, but
I'll trounce you just the same.

STRONGER ARGUMENT
I suppose you have one or two tricks up your sleeve?

WEAKER ARGUMENT
I do have a few progressive ideas.

STRONGER ARGUMENT
You're very trendy, aren't you,
(*indicating the audience*)
thanks to *these* idiots. They encourage you, while you corrupt the
young.

WEAKER ARGUMENT
Oh, please! These are the finest citizens in the world. They nurture
and encourage only what's best.

STRONGER ARGUMENT
It doesn't matter. I'll destroy you.

WEAKER ARGUMENT
Please! You're making me sick. Someone bring me a bucket!

STRONGER ARGUMENT

I can't bear to look at you.

WEAKER ARGUMENT

Relic!

STRONGER ARGUMENT

Freeloader!

WEAKER ARGUMENT

Buffoon!

STRONGER ARGUMENT

Bum-fucker!

WEAKER ARGUMENT

What a sweet compliment.

STRONGER ARGUMENT

You're shameless!

WEAKER ARGUMENT

You're archaic!

STRONGER ARGUMENT

It's arguments like you that give schooling a bad name.

CHORUS

Trusting their skill in oratory,
Each Argument will tell its story.
A chattering fox, a prattling fool,
It's hard to know if either's cruel.

Which one belongs to the Socratic cult?
We'll soon learn the end result.
Fearless, impudent, audacious, contestable,
Which Argument is the most detestable?

WEAKER ARGUMENT

Now, if I've got things *straight*, all I have to do is show that Strepsiades, here, is in a more advantageous position. Since, although he hasn't yet been screwed, everyone else has. Is that right?

STRONGER ARGUMENT

That's right.

WEAKER ARGUMENT

And if I defeat you on this point?

STRONGER ARGUMENT

Then I'll concede.

WEAKER ARGUMENT

So tell me, what do you think of our bankers?

STRONGER ARGUMENT

Talk about being screwed! The wealthy pay them to take it up the ass every day.

WEAKER ARGUMENT

Quite right. And our lawyers?

STRONGER ARGUMENT

Oh, please. They're the same. Only *more* so.

WEAKER ARGUMENT

What about our tragic dramatists?

STRONGER ARGUMENT

You couldn't find a bigger group of bum-lovers if you tried.

WEAKER ARGUMENT

I agree. And our moralists?

STRONGER ARGUMENT

Please. Have you ever met one who *didn't* enjoy taking it up the backside?

WEAKER ARGUMENT

I can't say that I have. And our politicians?

STRONGER ARGUMENT

Our politicians? They're all huge ass-kissers! *Enormous* ass-kissers!
*Gargantuan* ass-kissers!
   (*to a member of the audience*)
Am I right?

WEAKER ARGUMENT

All right. All right. Then don't you think it's time to admit you've
lost?

STRONGER ARGUMENT

What do you mean?

WEAKER ARGUMENT

Well, who's left? Take a look
   (*pointing at the audience*)
and tell me what you see.

STRONGER ARGUMENT

I'm looking.

WEAKER ARGUMENT

And?

STRONGER ARGUMENT

By all the gods! They're almost *all* ass-kissers!
   (*as he begins pointing out individual members of the audience*)
This man here is ... and this woman ... and that fellow over there
with the funny hair ... and you here ...
   (*blushing*)
Oh my!

WEAKER ARGUMENT

So what do you say now?

STRONGER ARGUMENT

   (*quietly*)
I have to concede.

#### WEAKER ARGUMENT
I'm sorry?

#### STRONGER ARGUMENT
I have to concede. You've proved your point. They're all screwed.

*As the* STRONGER ARGUMENT *exits in shame and the* WEAKER ARGUMENT *takes a bow, the* CHORUS *is worried.*

#### CHORUS
(*to the audience*)
The Weaker Argument has won the day!
Are we sure it's right to end this way?

#### STREPSIADES
(*to* SOCRATES)
Oh, yes, yes! That's exactly what I need you to teach my boy. For a moment there, you almost had me believing I was better off than I really am. You have to teach Pheidippides how you did that. How to make the Weaker Argument defeat the Stronger, that's what we need to know!

#### SOCRATES
Don't worry. He'll soon be a master of sophistry.

SOCRATES, PHEIDIPPIDES, *and the* WEAKER ARGUMENT *all exit into the School of Thinkology.*

#### STREPSIADES
At last! I can't thank Socrates enough. Soon I'll be delivered from my creditors and all will be well!

STREPSIADES *exits. As the* SUN *and* MOON *rotate by, the* CHORUS *indicates the passing of several days.*

#### CHORUS
Day.
Followed by night.
Followed by day.
Followed by night.
Followed by day.

*THE SCHOOL OF THINKOLOGY on the edge of Athens. Several days later.* STREPSIADES *enters.*

STREPSIADES

(*to the audience*)
My debts are due soon. And the bailiffs won't give me any more time. I've begged them to extend my credit. But all they want is their money. And if I don't pay, they say they'll sue! The greedy buggers.

(*approaching the School of Thinkology*)
Well, let them take me to court, that's what I say. If my Pheidippides has learned to talk that infuriating wisdom-lover's talk, they'll be sorry.

STREPSIADES *knocks on the door. The door opens and* SOCRATES *appears.*

SOCRATES

Strepsiades. Good to see you.

STREPSIADES

The same to you, mate! So tell me, has my boy learned that special way of arguing?

SOCRATES

He certainly has.

STREPSIADES

Oh, Queen of Quarrels, what terrific news!

SOCRATES

Now you'll be able to go to court and win, any time you want.

STREPSIADES

Even if there were witnesses?

SOCRATES

Even if there were a thousand witnesses!

PHEIDIPPIDES *enters from within the School of Thinkology.*

SOCRATES (*cont'd*)
Here's the young man you're looking for.

STREPSIADES
My boy! My *son*! I can't tell you how proud I am!

*As the* CHORUS *performs,* SOCRATES *re-enters the School of Thinkology, closing the door behind him.*

CHORUS
Here's a boy whose mind's now sharp,
Prepared to argue the unjust part.
His father thinks in desperate measures,
And asks his son to protect his treasures.

But there's more to life than a clever mind,
More to justice than ties that bind.
After listening to his fine new son,
He'll soon wish that he was dumb!

STREPSIADES
At last! Now we'll be able to avoid our debts. With your new skill at bamboozling creditors, we'll soon be living on Easy Street.

PHEIDIPPIDES
Maybe. If that's what I choose to do.

STREPSIADES
What in heaven are you babbling about?

PHEIDIPPIDES
You want me to act on your behalf. And I may. Or I may not. Now that I've been properly educated, I'm able to see an entire range of possibilities I never noticed before.

STREPSIADES
I'm still your father. It's only right that you do what I tell you!

PHEIDIPPIDES
'Only right'? Don't you know there's no difference between right

and wrong? I may decide to help you. Or I may not. Or, if I tire of hearing you prattle on like a child, I may decide to beat you.

STREPSIADES

What on earth are you saying? You wouldn't dare raise a hand against your father!

PHEIDIPPIDES

Of course I would. And my mother too. And I'd be perfectly justified in giving you both a sound thrashing.

STREPSIADES

How could it ever be right to beat your parents?

PHEIDIPPIDES

It's easy enough to prove.

STREPSIADES

(to the audience)
This is unbelievable! And to think that I paid to have him educated to argue like this.

CHORUS

You've got some work to do, old man,
You've got to get the upper hand.
You sent your son away to school,
To prove to all that you're no fool.

But now he's learned to argue and win,
Even against his honourable kin.
He has an argument he thinks will work,
Or he wouldn't be such a jerk.

STREPSIADES

(to PHEIDIPPIDES)
There's no way it could ever be right for a son to beat his parents.

PHEIDIPPIDES

Didn't you send me to school to learn to argue the unjust part?

STREPSIADES

Well, yes. But this can't be right.
(*to the audience*)
Although I have to admit, I am a little curious.
(*to* PHEIDIPPIDES)
Go on. Let's hear what you have to say.
(*mockingly*)
I can't wait.


PHEIDIPPIDES

(*pompously*)
Let me first say how grateful I am to you for allowing me to be educated by Socrates. When I was concentrating on my horses and chariots, I couldn't say three words without displaying my ignorance. But now I'm proficient in all the subtlest forms of argument. In fact, I have all the skills necessary to demonstrate any point I may want to advance – including the claim that I'd be perfectly justified in disciplining you.


STREPSIADES

(*angrily*)
You're treading a narrow path, my boy.


PHEIDIPPIDES

(*condescendingly*)
Maybe. But that's a separate matter. Do try to stay focused. Now, tell me: did you ever hit me when I was a child?


STREPSIADES

Of course. But only because I cared for you. Don't you remember? When you lisped your first words, I listened 'til I recognized every one. When you began to walk, I was there to see that you didn't fall. And when you went astray, I corrected you. But I always had your best interest at heart.


PHEIDIPPIDES

So if I 'care for you,' and if I have 'your best interest at heart,' I should be able to beat you, too. How could your body be protected against beatings, but not mine? Weren't we both born free men?

STREPSIADES

Well yes, but –


PHEIDIPPIDES

(*interrupting*)
I suppose you're going to say that the law permits this with children, but not with adults. But everyone knows that the elderly
have all entered into their 'second childhood.'


STREPSIADES

But, you see –


PHEIDIPPIDES

(*interrupting*)
So it's only right that you be beaten even more severely than I was,
since this is your second time 'round.


STREPSIADES

But there's not a city in the world where it's legal for a son to beat
his parents!


PHEIDIPPIDES

But it's just men like you and me who make the laws. So what's
preventing us from making a new law that says sons can beat their
parents? And if there's a delay in its enactment, we'll make it retro-
active so that even beatings given before the law was passed will
be legal!


STREPSIADES

(*to the audience*)
You know, friends, I'm beginning to think he may have a point.
Should I concede that the law is just whatever we want it to be?
(*to a father in the audience*)
That men our age should be able to be punished by our sons? That
can't be right. That damned Socrates and his Weaker Argument,
corrupting the young! He'll be the end of us all!


CHORUS

You thought it nice
To worship vice.

But now you've learned
And become concerned.

STREPSIADES

(*to the* CHORUS)
Oh I have, Chorus. I have. But what can I do?

CHORUS

Your son seems keen to argue this way,
So perhaps his logic will win the day.
If so, it's time to admit defeat,
And abandon the crooked path of deceit!

STREPSIADES

(*to the* CHORUS)
You're right, Chorus. I never should have tried to escape my debts.
And I never should have listened to Socrates!

*As* STREPSIADES *speaks,* STUDENTS *begin exiting the School of Thinkology to return to their families.* PHEIDIPPIDES *greets many of them as they pass him on their way home.*

STREPSIADES (*cont'd*)

(*to the audience*)
Look at all the young people he's corrupted. Heading home to ... to who knows what? To avoid paying their debts? To beat *their* parents? This can't be right. Young men and women should be educated at home. Not by these money-grubbing philosophers. And husbands and wives should be grateful they have each other to lean on as they raise their children.

CHORUS

(*to the audience*)
Is there justice in old age?
Can a father contain his rage?
Is education a matter of might?
Or should a school teach what's right!

STREPSIADES *picks up an axe.*

STREPSIADES

We all know what needs to be done.
  (*indicating his axe*)
It's time for Socrates to be paid his tuition in full! I'm going to pick
an argument with his school all right. And if he tries to intervene,
I'll show him the point of my axe!

CHORUS

Now it's time to end our play,
We've sung enough for you today.

Goodbye!

*INTERMISSION*

# Act Two
## *Apology*

LEADER OF THE CHORUS

Almost a quarter century after Aristophanes' *Clouds* was first performed, Socrates was charged with corrupting the young and failing to recognize the traditional Greek gods. His trial was held just over 2,400 years ago, in 399 BCE.

Because the trial took place not long after the end of the Peloponnesian War, Athens' humiliating loss to Sparta was still on many people's minds. During wartime, it was understood that victory came from two sources: the protection of the gods, and the unwavering loyalty of a city's young soldiers. So the charge of corrupting the young and failing to recognize the city's gods was serious, and much like the charge of treason.

At his trial, Socrates was charged by three men: Meletus, Anytus, and Lykon. In an Athenian court there were no lawyers. The accusers and the accused spoke for themselves. So after hearing from his accusers, Socrates had to give a speech in his own defence. It's this speech we're going to hear next.

Following the speech, it will be your job as jurors to decide Socrates' guilt or innocence. After he completes his speech, you'll be asked to walk to the front of the theatre to vote. Be sure to exercise your vote wisely.

There's one other thing: Athenian juries weren't quiet. If people thought a speaker was stretching or misrepresenting the truth, they'd often yell out. So if you hear others heckling, you're welcome to join in!

We join the proceedings just as Socrates is being presented to the jury.

*THE AREOPAGUS near the centre of Athens. Day. Seated behind a table is an* ARCHON *(or magistrate) together with several* DIGNITARIES. *On the table is the written indictment against Socrates. Also onstage are Socrates' three accusers –* MELETUS, ANYTUS, *and* LYKON *– as well as* SOCRATES *and a* GUARD. MELETUS, ANYTUS, LYKON, *and the* DIGNITARIES *are talking among themselves.*

*The* ARCHON *stands and raises his hand. Everyone becomes quiet. The* GUARD *presents* SOCRATES *to the jury. The* ARCHON *sits and the* GUARD *withdraws.*

### SOCRATES

Well, men of Athens, I don't know whether you've been persuaded by my accusers. But I have to admit, they spoke pretty convincingly.
(*jokingly*)
So convincingly, they *almost* convinced *me*!

But hardly a word of what they said was true!

What amazed me most was when they said you had to be careful not to let me trick you because I'm such a clever speaker. They should be ashamed of themselves! As soon as I open my mouth, it'll be obvious that I'm not a clever speaker –
(*jokingly*)
Unless by a 'clever speaker' they mean someone who speaks the truth. If that's what they mean, then I have to admit, I'm a much more clever speaker than they are.

But I'm not like them. They tell you either nothing that's true, or only partial truths. From me, what you'll get is the truth, the whole truth, and nothing but the truth.

And my words won't be gussied up the way theirs are, with lots of verbs and nouns. My speech won't be filled with 'legalese.' I'll just speak with whatever words come to mind.

All I ask is that you listen to me. Don't be put off if you hear me talk the same way I do in the marketplace. You've all heard me there. That's how I am. I was born seventy years ago and this is the first time I've been in a court of law. So the talk here is foreign to me.

### MELETUS

(*to* LYKON *and* ANYTUS)
He's frightened! He's already making excuses.

SOCRATES

(*to* MELETUS)

Look, all I'm saying is that if a foreigner showed up here, you'd bear with him if he spoke the way he did in his hometown. So I'm just asking that, however I talk – whether it's plain or fancy – look to see if I'm telling the truth.

(*to the jury*)

Because the same thing is good for a speaker *and* a juror: the truth.

People have been coming to you with accusations about me for a long time now. So it's probably best if I start by speaking against the old accusations first, and then against the new ones. I worry about my old accusers even more than

(*pointing to* MELETUS)

Meletus and his friends. They got to you in your childhood, when you were young and impressionable.

You remember Aristophanes' play, don't you?

(*sarcastically*)

There's supposed to be this Socrates, a wise man, who thinks about things up in the sky and under the ground, and who doesn't believe in the gods. And he makes weak arguments appear to be strong.

(*seriously*)

Members of the jury, the people who've spread these rumours – they're my real accusers. And you know how rumours are! You never know who said what. There's no one to argue with – it's like fighting shadows!

So I have two different kinds of accusers.

(*pointing to* MELETUS, ANYTUS, *and* LYKON)

Some accuse me now. Others have been accusing me for a long time. And you can see that I have to defend myself against the first ones first, because you heard them first.

Of course, I only have a short time to make my case. But I hope I'll succeed. That would be good for me, and for you.

(*jokingly*)

Although it would better for me, of course.

It's going to be difficult, and I don't want to lose sight of that. But one way or another, it'll be as the gods want it. My job is just to do what's right.

So let's start at the beginning. What are my accusers saying? Well,

(*picking up the written indictment from in front of the* ARCHON)
if you want to know the *formal* charges, you have to read the indictment.

(*waving, but not reading, the indictment*)
But my *original* accusers said that I look under the ground and up
in the sky. And that I make weak words appear to be strong.

(*throwing down the indictment*)
Or something like that. That's what you saw in that play by Aristophanes.

(*sarcastically*)
A 'Socrates' swings in from the clouds and says, 'I can walk on air,'
and then he fools around with some other nonsense that I don't
have a clue about. And doesn't he teach some poor boy some kind
of foolishness? I don't know about you, but the whole thing left my
head spinning.

(*as an afterthought*)
Although I suppose the acting was pretty good.

I don't say it's dishonourable to know things like that – oops,
maybe I shouldn't say that. I don't want to give Meletus grounds
for any new charges. Let me just say that I'm not into things like
that.

(*approaching the jury*)
Most of you can serve as witnesses for me. If you've heard that
I've run a school, or that I've taught people for money, you know
that's not true.

Don't get me wrong. People who can teach the way Gorgias of
Leontini, Prodikos of Ceos, and Hippias of Elis can – they're great
men. They can go anywhere they want. And wherever they go,
they can convince young men – who could be with anyone – to
leave the people they're with and be with them. And they can convince their parents to pay them for the privilege, and be grateful
for it too.

I myself saw a man from Paros. He's wise this way. And there's
this other man I know who pays him for his wisdom. In fact, he
pays him more than all the other sophists put together.

CALLIAS *enters.*

SOCRATES (*cont'd*)
His name is Callias. He's the son of Hipponicus. Well, I went to

him and I said, 'Callias' – he has two sons – 'Callias,' I said, 'if your two sons were horses or bulls, we'd take them to someone who knew how to make them fine and good, as befits a horse or a bull.'

CALLIAS

We would.

SOCRATES

'And we'd pay for this, too. We'd take them to some kind of farmer or horseman.'

SOME HECKLERS

We're people, not animals!

SOCRATES

(*to the* HECKLERS)
That's what *I* said!
(*to* CALLIAS)
'But your sons aren't animals,' I said to him. 'They're people. So who has the knowledge people need? Who knows about virtue and excellence, so he can teach your sons? I take it that, having two sons, you've thought about this. Is there anyone?' I asked him, 'or not?'

He looked me straight in the eye, and he said:

CALLIAS

Of course there's someone.

SOCRATES

'Who?' I asked him. 'Where does he come from and how much does he charge?'

CALLIAS

His name is Evenus. He's from Paros and he charges 500 drachmas.

SOCRATES

Five hundred drachmas! Wow! If this Evenus can really teach people to do what's right, and if he charges so little for it, he's truly a great man. If I knew how to teach people that sort of thing, I'd be so

proud there'd be no living with me!
   But I don't, men of Athens.

LYKON

(to MELETUS and ANYTUS)
That's the truth.

CALLIAS exits.

SOCRATES
(pointing to MELETUS, ANYTUS, and LYKON)
So why have these men charged me? Why do people think I put on
airs and try to pretend I'm wise when I'm not?

   I'll tell you. But you have to listen carefully, because otherwise
you may think I'm just fooling around. But I'm not.

   I admit that over the years I've acquired a reputation for having
a certain kind of wisdom. And in *one sense*, perhaps I really am
wise.

MELETUS

Here we go.

ANYTUS

He's a liar! A liar!

LYKON

(to the jury, overlapping)
We warned you! We warned you!

SOME HECKLERS

(overlapping)
Liar! Liar!

ARCHON

Quiet!

SOCRATES

Please! Men of Athens! Don't get angry with me. I don't want you
to think it's me who's making these claims. I have the word of
a witness – a witness I know you'll trust. As a witness to my wisdom – such as it is – I offer the god at Delphi.

SOME HECKLERS

Liar! Liar!

SOME HECKLERS

(*overlapping*)
Blasphemy! Blasphemy!

ARCHON

Let him speak.

SOCRATES

You know Chaerephon. He's been my friend since childhood. He's been a friend to many of you, too. He left the city with you when you had to flee during the war, and came back when you came back.

Well, you know how Chaerephon was. Whatever he did, he did to the extreme. So, when he went to Delphi he was brave enough to approach the Oracle –

SOME HECKLERS

(*interrupting*)
Liar! Liar!

SOME HECKLERS

(*interrupting*)
He didn't! Never!

SOCRATES

(*to the* HECKLERS)
Look, don't get excited. I'm just repeating what others will tell you. He approached the Oracle and asked if anyone was wiser than me. The priestess answered that no one was wiser than Socrates. His brother can be a witness to this, if you like, since Chaerephon's now dead.

ANYTUS

Pretty convenient.

SOCRATES

I'm not proud of this. All I want to do is show you where these attacks against me have come from. Why would the god say what he said? Maybe he was speaking in riddles? I didn't have the faintest idea I was wise. So why would the Oracle say I was the wisest?

MELETUS

Why indeed.

SOCRATES

I thought about it for a long time. I began to work very hard to find a way to understand it.

*Several* POLITICIANS *enter.*

SOCRATES (*cont'd*)
(*indicating the* POLITICIANS)
I went to someone who had a reputation for being wise, and I thought, 'I'll test the prophecy and show the Oracle: Look, you said I was the wisest, but here's someone wiser than me.'

Well, I examined the person I went to – I don't need to tell you his name, it's enough to say he was one of our politicians, a very wise man – and I talked with him. But it turned out he really wasn't very wise. So I tried to show him that, even though he *thought* he was wise, he wasn't.

Well, he and the people around him began to get angry with me.

SOME HECKLERS

No! Surely not!

SOME HECKLERS

Liar! Liar!

SOME HECKLERS

(*overlapping*)
Shh! Shh! Be quiet!

SOCRATES

It's true. I think they even began to hate me. But I started to think, maybe I *am* wiser than that man. There's no risk that either of us knows anything important. But he *thinks* he knows something and doesn't. So even though I don't know much, at least I don't think I do when I don't.

Then I went to another politician who was said to be wiser still, and he seemed to me to be the same. And then he hated me, too. And so did all his friends.

*The* POLITICIANS *exit.*

SOCRATES (*cont'd*)
(*focusing on an individual jury member*)
I have to make you understand how *obligated* I felt to make these inquiries. Because of what the god had said, I really felt I had to test people, especially those with a reputation for wisdom.

*Several* POETS *enter.*

SOCRATES (*cont'd*)
(*indicating the* POETS)
So, after I'd examined the politicians, I went to the poets, who write songs and tragedies, and I asked them, 'Why do you write what you do?' hoping to learn something from them.

Well, I'm ashamed to tell you what I discovered. Still, I have to say it: almost anyone would have been able to explain their poetry better than they could. All I learned was that poetry was somehow 'in their nature.' When they did it,
(*sarcastically*)
it was as if they were 'out of their minds,' like people who see gods and make prophecies. People like that don't know what they're talking about, even if they think they do.

*The* POETS *exit.*

SOCRATES (*cont'd*)
So I left the poets, realizing that I'd come out on top, just as I had with the politicians.

*Several* CRAFTSMEN *enter.*

SOCRATES (*cont'd*)
(*indicating the* CRAFTSMEN)
Finally, I went to the craftsmen. I thought that from them at least, I'd learn some good things – and I wasn't disappointed. They did

know things about their crafts, and in a sense, they really were wise.

But, once again the same thing that was true of the poets and the politicians was true of the craftsmen. Because they could produce technically fine work, each of them thought they knew other things too – big, important things, things you'd have to be really wise to know. But they didn't.

So I asked myself, on behalf of the Oracle, 'Would I be better off knowing what they know, but also thinking I was wise when I wasn't? Or not?' My answer was that I wouldn't be.

*The* CRAFTSMEN *exit.*

SOCRATES (*cont'd*)

But because of my questions, a lot of people began to fling accusations at me, and some people said I was wise, even though I'm not.

What I learned is that only the gods have real wisdom. There's very little human wisdom, and what there is, isn't worth much. So when the god said I was the wisest, he was just using my name as a kind of stand-in, saying that it's people like me, who don't claim to know much, who know the most, because they're not mistaken about what they believe.

Anyway, because of all the work I've done on behalf of the god, I haven't had any free time to spend on public affairs, or even on my *own* affairs. I've ended up being totally poor. But I've tried my best to do the god's bidding.

ANYTUS

(*to the jury*)
Don't believe him.

LYKON

(*overlapping*)
He's a liar.

MELETUS

We told you.

SOCRATES

Oh, there's one other thing. It's true. Young men have sometimes followed me around. Particularly young men with time on their hands. They like to hear people being taken down a peg, and they sometimes try to imitate me, just for fun.

MELETUS

He admits it!

LYKON

(*to the jury*)
Do you hear him?

SOME HECKLERS

We do.

SOCRATES

But this isn't *my* fault. They find there's no shortage of people who think they know something when really they don't. Then people become angry with me, and say I'm 'corrupting the young.'

If someone asks them how I do this, they haven't got a clue. But not wanting to seem stuck, they say I don't believe in the gods, and that I make the weaker argument appear to be the stronger.

SOME HECKLERS

Shame! Shame!

SOCRATES

(*to the* HECKLERS)
It *is* shameful. The upshot is that Meletus and Anytus and Lykon have brought these charges against me. Meletus for the poets,
(*with incredulity*)
who hate me. Anytus for the politicians,
(*with resignation*)
who hate me. And Lykon for the orators,
(*with boredom*)
who also hate me. So now I have to defend myself against them and their charges. So let's look at what they say.
(*picking up and reading from the indictment*)
They say I 'wrongfully corrupt the young' –
(*shaking his head*)
As if someone else might *rightfully* corrupt them. And that I don't

believe 'in the gods the city believes in.' And that I 'make up new divine things.'

(*tossing down the indictment*)

Something like that. The bottom line is they think I'm corrupting the young, when really it's Meletus who's doing something wrong. He's playing around with something very serious. He's pretending to care about something he doesn't care about at all.

SOME HECKLERS

How do you know? How do you know?

SOCRATES

(*to the jury members*)

How do I know? I'll show you.

(*to* MELETUS)

Meletus, come here. These jurymen want to hear what you have to say.

MELETUS

I've already said what I have to say.

SOCRATES

Then it won't hurt you to say it again, will it?

MELETUS *reluctantly approaches* SOCRATES.

SOCRATES (*cont'd*)

You think education's important, do you?

MELETUS

Of course I do.

SOCRATES

All right, then. Tell us who can teach our young people the most.

MELETUS

I don't know what you mean.

SOCRATES

Come on. You must have thought about this, or you wouldn't have charged me. If I'm the one who's corrupting them, who's improving them?

MELETUS *gives no answer.*

SOCRATES *(cont'd)*
*(to the jury)*
You see, he doesn't know.
*(to* MELETUS)
You should be ashamed of yourself. I don't think you've given a moment's thought to what makes a good education.

MELETUS
Of course I have. It's the laws that teach us what's right.

SOCRATES
Ohhh! 'The laws.' But that's not what I asked. I asked you *who* – what person – is capable of teaching our young people what's right.

MELETUS
*(pointing to the jury)*
These people, Socrates. This jury can.

SOCRATES
Do you mean *these* people, Meletus? These are the ones who know how to educate our young?

MELETUS
That's right.

SOCRATES
Is it all of them, or only some of them?

MELETUS
Every one of them.

SOCRATES
Wow! This is great news. And are there others too? What about the men and women who're here today who aren't members of the jury?

MELETUS

They all know what's right, too.

SOCRATES

And what about everyone else?

MELETUS

(*in frustration*)
Everyone! Everyone in Athens knows how to educate the young,
except you!

SOCRATES

Hmmm. So it seems that every Athenian is able to educate our
young people, except me.
(*incredulously*)
*I'm* the only one who corrupts them? Is that what you're saying?

MELETUS

For someone who's supposed to be smart, you've *finally* understood the charge.

SOCRATES

All right then, Meletus. To hear you tell it, I must be a very, very,
*very* bad man.
  But tell me this: do you think the same is true of animals? Is it
true that almost everyone knows how to train a good horse? And
that only one person doesn't?
  Or isn't it the other way 'round? Aren't there really only a few
people who're able to train a horse properly? And if this is true of
horses, isn't it even more true of people?

MELETUS *gives no answer.*

SOCRATES (*cont'd*)

(*to the jury*)
You see? He hasn't given a moment's thought to what makes a
good education.

SOME HECKLERS

Shame! Shame!

SOCRATES

(*to* MELETUS)

Here's an easier question. Is it better to live among good people or bad?

MELETUS *is confused.*

SOCRATES (*cont'd*)

Come on, it's not a hard question. Would you rather live among people who don't know right from wrong? Who steal from you, and do other bad things? Or not?

MELETUS *looks to* LYKON *and* ANYTUS.

SOCRATES (*cont'd*)

Come on, Mr Know-It-All. The law says you have to answer.

ARCHON

(*to* MELETUS)

It does.

SOCRATES

So would you prefer to live among bad people? Or not?

MELETUS

No, of course not.

SOCRATES

So why do you think I'm any different? Why would I corrupt the young, knowing that I'd have to live with them?

(*in frustration*)

It doesn't make any sense. Am I so stupid that I don't know that if I make people bad, I run the risk that they'll do bad things to me? I don't think you'll be able to convince the jury I'm *that* stupid. And even if I was, I'd need to be educated, not punished.

ANYTUS

(*to* LYKON)

Like there's a difference.

SOCRATES

You also say I don't believe in the city's gods, but in some new-fangled divinities instead. Is that right?

MELETUS

That's right. New gods that don't even have names. And that's
why the real gods have abandoned us.

SOCRATES

But how can this be? Are you saying that I'm not like other men?
That I don't think the sun and moon are gods?

MELETUS

That's right.
    (*to the jury*)
He says the sun is a rock and the moon is dirt!

SOCRATES

Whoa! Hold your horses, Meletus. Who do you think is on trial
here? Anaxagoras? Do you think so little of these jurors? Do you
think they're illiterate? That's Anaxagoras' view.
    (*to the jury*)
Any bookseller will sell you his book for a drachma or two if you
want to check.
    (*to* MELETUS)
So what are you trying to do? Make me into a joke? Are you saying
I just put forward the weird ideas of others, as if they were my
own?

MELETUS

Who knows what you do.

SOCRATES

Well, I don't. And now you say I don't believe in the gods at all?

MELETUS

That's right! Not at all.

SOCRATES

*And* that I also believe in some new kinds of divinities?

MELETUS

That's right! You don't believe in the real gods, only some made-up ones.

SOCRATES

I can't believe what you're saying, Meletus. I don't even think *you* could believe it.

(*to the jury*)

It's as if he's trying to make a puzzle for us: 'Will Socrates – this wise guy – will he know that I'm having fun with him and contradicting myself? Or will I fool him, and everyone else too?'

(*to* MELETUS)

You're contradicting your own indictment! It says I don't believe in the gods, and now you say I do believe in them!

MELETUS

Are you really this stupid? Not in *them*. Not in the *real* gods. Only in some silly new ones.

SOCRATES

But how could anyone believe in new gods without believing in the old ones? Everyone knows it's the old gods who give birth to new ones. Or more precisely, that new divinities are the offspring of the old gods together with nymphs, or

(*winking at an attractive woman in the gallery*)

with *especially* attractive women.

So how could anyone believe in the children of the gods and not in the gods? That would be as stupid as believing that horses and asses can have children – half-asses – and then not believing in horses or asses.

MELETUS

(*in frustration*)

Who knows what you believe!

SOCRATES

All I'm saying is that if I believed in these new divinities of yours, then I'd have to believe in their parents, too. So what are you trying to do? Trick us with your indictment?

(*to the jury*)
What a charlatan!

MELETUS

I might not be as tricky as you,
(*to the jury*)
but I'm not the one who taught Alcibiades and Critias and the
other traitors during the war. We lost that war! Because the gods –
the *real* gods – abandoned us. Young men don't just wake up one
morning and decide to become traitors. There has to be a reason.
And
(*pointing to* SOCRATES)
you're looking at him!

SOCRATES

Men of Athens, you can't trust anything he says! I've told you, I
never ran a school and I never taught people for money! In fact,
sometimes I even think virtue *can't* be taught!

ANYTUS

Maybe not. But wickedness can!

MELETUS

(*to the jury*)
You remember Alcibiades. He traded secrets with Sparta during
the war. And after the war, when he was dead, and when the Spartans wanted to set up their puppet regime here in Athens, who did
they turn to? Critias and the others. You remember.
(*pointing to* SOCRATES)
They were all *his* students!

*In contempt,* MELETUS *withdraws to join* ANYTUS *and* LYKON.

SOCRATES

This is nonsense! Anyone with even a smidgen of brains can see
that you should just let me go.
Now one of you on the jury *might* say:

JURYMAN

Socrates, if there isn't anything shameful about what you've been doing, why are you in such danger? This good jury might actually believe some of these charges. They may even decide to put you to death. Doesn't that worry you?

SOCRATES

If someone asked me this question, I'd have to answer truthfully. And truthfully, danger just isn't something we should take into account when we're trying to decide between right and wrong.

Remember the heroes at Troy? Remember when Achilles, the son of Thetis, knew it was his duty to kill Hector, regardless of the danger?

THETIS *and* ACHILLES *appear, as if in a vision.*

SOCRATES (*cont'd*)

His mother, being a god, said something like this to him:

THETIS

My son, if you avenge the murder of your friend Patroclus and kill Hector, you'll surely die. Behind Hector your future lies waiting.

SOCRATES

But this danger meant nothing to Achilles. He was much more afraid of living badly – of not avenging his friend – than he was of dying. So bang! Just like that, he said:

ACHILLES

Then let me die, having punished the wrongdoers. I'd rather face death than stay here beside the boats, a laughingstock, nothing more than a burden upon the ground.

SOCRATES

Do you think Achilles was worried about danger then? Hardly.

That's how it is, men of Athens. Once you discover what's right, you have to stick to it, regardless of the danger.

THETIS *and* ACHILLES *disappear.*

SOCRATES (*cont'd*)

That's how it was during the war when we stayed at our posts in

Potideia, in Amphipolis, and Delium. None of us ran away just because we'd become afraid of death, or some other trifle.

Being afraid of death is nothing more than thinking you're wise when you're not, thinking you know something you don't.

No one knows whether death is the end, or just a new beginning. But people fear death, as if they somehow knew it was the greatest of evils. If this isn't the stupidest thing a person could do – to think he knows something when he doesn't – then I don't know what is.

If there's one way in which I'm different from other people, it's that I don't pretend to know what happens after you die. None of us should pretend to know things we don't.

That's why I've spent so much time nagging you. It's as if Athens was a big, well-bred horse – so big, it's dopey, and needs a gadfly to pester it. It's been my job to nag you to do what's right. And if I die, you won't find someone else to take my place.

SOME HECKLERS

Good! We've had enough!

SOCRATES

So if you want my advice, you should just let me go.

MELETUS

Oh, please!

LYKON

Don't listen to him.

SOME HECKLERS

(*overlapping*)
Enough! We've heard enough!

SOCRATES

(*to the* HECKLERS)
Calm down! You know very well that if you kill me, and if I am what I say I am, then you'll be hurting yourself much more than you'll be hurting me.

(*pointing to* MELETUS, ANYTUS *and* LYKON)
These men can't hurt me. The only thing that can hurt a man is

damage to his character. A truly good man can *never* be harmed. And if that's right, you need me more than I need to live.

SOME HECKLERS

Please! This is unbelievable.

SOCRATES

Mark it down! I'm one of the gods' gifts to this city!

SOME HECKLERS

Unbelievable! Unbelievable!

SOCRATES

It's hardly human the way I've ignored my own needs, the way I've ignored my family – because I'm constantly worrying about *your* business, going to you privately, as a father or older brother might, and trying to convince you *to pay attention to virtue.*

Maybe it seems strange that, on the one hand, I go around advising people privately about things, but that I never get up in public to take part in the Assembly. But it's a good thing I haven't been involved in politics. If I had been, I'd probably have been killed years ago.

LYKON

It would have saved us the trouble!

SOCRATES

But if I'd been killed, I wouldn't have been of any use to you. Nobody can fight for justice *and* be involved in politics!

SOME HECKLERS

Liar! Liar!

SOME HECKLERS

(*overlapping*)
Unbelievable. Do you hear him?

SOCRATES

(*to the* HECKLERS)
Don't get angry with me! I have a couple of big proofs of this. The

kind you like: deeds, not words.

Listen to what happened to me. Then you'll know I haven't shied away from doing what's right, just because of a little danger.

You know I never held public office, except that one time when I was on the Council. It was when the eight generals were being tried for dereliction of duty after the battle at Arginusae. You remember. *You* wanted to condemn them all with one vote, rather than take a separate vote for each man. But trying them together was against the law.

Everyone agrees about this now. But at the time, *I* was the only one who stood up for the law. I wouldn't allow the vote to proceed, even though some of you said I should be charged with obstruction! You all went along with the mob, roaring like animals! But I followed the law. I risked being put in jail, or even being killed.

SOME HECKLERS

It's true. I remember.

SOCRATES

That was when the city was being run democratically. But when the Tyrants took control, it was just the same. They called us before them – there were five of us. They ordered us to bring Leon of Salamis back to Athens so they could kill him. They ordered a lot of people to do a lot of things like that. They wanted to involve as many people in their illegal actions as they could, to taint us all, so no one would complain.

But that time, too, I showed you. Not in words, but in deeds. I showed you that death means nothing to me. The other four went off to Salamis and brought Leon back. But I just went home. If the Tyrants hadn't fallen soon afterwards, I would have been executed.

SOME HECKLERS

It's true. It's true. I remember.

SOCRATES

So if I *had* been involved in politics, do you think I'd have survived long? Not likely. Nor would any other man. Not if he cares about justice.

SOME HECKLERS
Unbelievable! Unbelievable!


SOCRATES
It's the common man – not the great kings and politicians – who finds it easiest to stay out of trouble. No tragic poet has even had the audacity to end his play with the slaughter of the Chorus!

So why do young men enjoy wasting their time with me? You've already heard the answer. They like to hang around me because it's fun to see someone who thinks he's smart get taken down a peg.

But if anyone's been corrupted as a result of this, don't you think he'd complain? Or that his father or brothers would? Wouldn't they get up now and accuse me, and demand that I get what I deserve? There are lots of them here.

(pointing)
There's Crito. He's known me all my life and he's the father of Critobulus. And

(pointing)
there's Lysanias the Sphettian, the father of Aeschines.

(pointing)
Nicostratus is here – the son of Theozotides and the brother of Theodotus. Of course, Theodotus has died, so he can't tell us what he thinks. But

(pointing)
there's Adeimantos, the son of Ariston,

(pointing)
whose brother Plato is also here. And there are plenty of others too. Don't you think that, among them,

(with condescension, pointing to MELETUS)
Meletus should be able to find at least *one* witness to back up what he's said?


SOCRATES *pauses. There's no response.*


SOCRATES (cont'd)
I didn't think so. No, it's just the opposite. Everybody is ready to help me. Me, the one who's been charged with 'corrupting the young.'

Well, that's pretty much all I have to say. Some of you might think I should do as others do, and beg the jury with floods of tears, and bring forward my wife and children to create as much pity as I can. But I won't.

JURYMAN

Why not? Doesn't our decision matter to you?

SOCRATES

Why not? It's not because I don't have a family. As Homer says, 'I didn't spring from a rock or a tree.' And it's not because I'm brave in the face of death. Or out of any disrespect to you. It just wouldn't be right.

Trials are meant to be places of reason and deliberation. Not soap operas. Jurors don't dispense justice as a charity. Or as a reward for a good performance.

You're about to make a judgement. You've sworn an oath to *judge*, not by what gives you pleasure, but in accordance with the truth and the law. So it's important that we respect justice. And the gods.

Throughout my life, I've always tried to do what's right. I've also never misled the young. And I believe in the gods even more than my accusers do.

So the only thing I hope is that you – and the gods – will judge me in a way that's best for us all.

*The* GUARD *accompanies* SOCRATES *offstage.* MELETUS, ANYTUS, *and* LYKON *follow.*

ARCHON

Members of the jury, you're now required to cast your votes. Please rise.

*The audience members stand.*

ARCHON (*cont'd*)

If you believe Socrates should be found guilty of corrupting the young, you're to select a black stone and place it in the bronze container. If you think he's not guilty, you're to select a white stone.

Remember: black means guilty, white means not guilty.

*The audience members vote and return to their seats. When the voting is complete, the* ARCHON *and* DIGNITARIES *take the votes and go offstage.*

*After a short time,* MELETUS, ANYTUS, *and* LYKON *return.* SOCRATES *and the* GUARD *return. The* ARCHON *and* DIGNITARIES *return.*

ARCHON

The votes have been counted. Socrates has been found guilty of corrupting the young!

SOME HECKLERS

Yes! Yes!

SOME HECKLERS

*(overlapping)*
No! No!

SOCRATES

Men of Athens! Please! I'm not upset about what's happened. It's not a big surprise. The amazing thing is how close the vote was. I thought I'd lose by far more than this. If only thirty votes had gone the other way, I'd have been acquitted.

In fact, if you want my opinion, as far as Meletus is concerned, I think I *have* been acquitted. If Anytus and Lykon hadn't joined him in bringing the charges against me, he'd have had to pay a 1,000-drachma fine for making a frivolous charge.

MELETUS

Oh, please! You're guilty. *You're guilty!* Admit it!

ARCHON

Enough. Both sides have to propose penalties.

ANYTUS *and* LYKON *want to confer with* MELETUS, *but* MELETUS *barges ahead.*

MELETUS

Death! The prosecution demands death!

ANYTUS

Or banishment!

MELETUS

No! Death!

SOCRATES

(*laughing*)
So Meletus thinks I should be put to death. What counter-proposal
should I make? What punishment do I deserve?

SOME HECKLERS

Nothing! Nothing!

SOME HECKLERS

(*overlapping*)
Death! Death!

SOME HECKLERS

(*overlapping*)
A fine! A fine!

SOCRATES

Perhaps I *should* pay a fine. But why? Why should I pay for having
tried to help you be your best?

I know! Someone who helps you the way I do should get all his
meals for free at City Hall! Don't you think I deserve this more
than some guy who wins a horse race at the Olympics? He *seems* to
make you happy, but I *make* you happy. And he doesn't need the
food. But I do.

LYKON

Not for long!

SOCRATES

If it's a question of what I *deserve*, then my punishment should be
that I get to eat all my meals for free.

SOME HECKLERS

Shame! Shame!

SOME HECKLERS

(*overlapping*)
Death! Death!

MELETUS

(*to the* ARCHON)
Make him be serious!

SOCRATES

Oh. Maybe it sounds like I'm begging you for something I don't deserve. But that's not what I meant. It's just that I haven't done anything wrong. You don't believe this, but that's only because we've had so little time to talk about things.

If the laws here were the same as elsewhere, and you allowed the court more than just one day to decide matters of life or death, I'd have convinced you. But since I haven't done anything wrong, I'd be doing myself an injustice if I said I deserved something bad when I don't.

(*to the jury, but facing* MELETUS)

Should I be *afraid* of the punishment Meletus wants to give me? Me? Someone who doesn't know whether death is good or bad? Should I choose instead something I *know* is bad?

(*turning to face the jury*)

Should I give you some money to escape, as if paying a fine would make you change your mind about me?

I suppose some of you might accept banishment as a punishment. But where would I go? What kind of life would I have, at my age, going from place to place, just to be chased out of one city after another?

I can just see it. Wherever I went, the young people would flock around me so they could listen to what I had to say. If I made them go away, they'd convince their parents to kick me out of town. And if I didn't make them go away, the old people would kick me out anyway, to protect their children.

So you're stuck with me.

Of course, some of you might prefer that I just go home and be quiet. I can imagine you asking me:

JURYMAN

Socrates, if we make it a condition of your release, will you promise to stop going around nagging people? Will you promise to stop influencing the young with your strange ideas?

SOCRATES

(*with regret*)

Unfortunately this is something I just can't do. Refusing to examine what's right would mean abandoning everything that's important. I know you'll think I'm being ironic, but the greatest thing a man can do is test himself and others against the good. I mean it when I say the unexamined life is not worth living.

So we're back to the question of punishment. If I had some money, I wouldn't mind paying a fine. But I don't have much. If you want to know what I can pay, well, I can pay one piece of silver.

LYKON

Please!

PLATO

(*from the gallery*)
Three thousand drachmas!

ARCHON

What?

CRITO

(*from the gallery*)
He said 3,000 drachmas. We'll guarantee it.

SOCRATES

Oh, Plato, who's sitting over there, and Crito and Critobulus and Apollodorus – they say I should put the fine at 3,000 drachmas. They're good for it. So, all right, that's what I'll say my penalty should be: 3,000 drachmas.

*The* ARCHON *and* DIGNITARIES *confer among themselves and reach a decision.*

ARCHON

The penalty is death.

MELETUS, ANYTUS, *and* LYKON *stand up and congratulate each other. They begin preparing to leave.*

SOME HECKLERS

No! No!

SOME HECKLERS

(*overlapping*)
Yes! Yes! Well done!

SOCRATES

(*to the* HECKLERS)

Please! Men of Athens, please! There's nothing to get excited about. Although if you'd waited a little longer, you would've got the same result without all this trouble. I'm an old man. I would have died soon anyway.

MELETUS, ANYTUS, *and* LYKON *leave.*

SOCRATES (*cont'd*)

If any of you want to stay awhile, I do have a few more things to say. I don't want you to think that I regret the speech I gave, or the way I gave it. I know some of you think that if I'd been more humble, I could've gone free.

But the real problem is that I wasn't brazen enough to say what you wanted me to say. The only thing that would have made you happy was to hear me crying and carrying on, saying things that are beneath me. That's what you've seen others do.

But a little danger shouldn't make us act like cowards. It's much more difficult praising the Athenians in Sparta than in Athens. Even now I don't regret the speech I gave. I'd much rather die, having given that speech, than live any other way.

Nobody should try to run from death at any cost – not in court, not in war, not anywhere. It's obvious that even in battle there are plenty of ways to escape death. You can drop your weapons and run. You can turn around and plead with whoever's chasing you. And there are other ways too, if you're 'courageous' enough to do or say *anything*.

No, my friends, it's not hard to escape death. It's much harder to escape wickedness. Wickedness runs faster than death.

Since I'm old and slow, I've been caught by the slow one. But my accusers, being clever and sharp, have escaped the slow one, only to be caught by evil.

So now, it's time for me to leave, since you've decided that I need to pay the fine of death.

*The* ARCHON, DIGNITARIES, *and* GUARD *begin to confer among themselves.*

SOCRATES (*cont'd*)

(*indicating the* ARCHON, DIGNITARIES, *and* GUARD)

But as long as they're busy, I want to say a few words to those of you who voted for my acquittal. Stay with me a while. Nothing prevents us from swapping a few stories.

(*intimately*)

And since we're close, I want to tell you something.

My friends, something amazing has happened to me. Normally, in the past, if I were going to do something that I wasn't supposed to, I'd receive a warning from one of the gods telling me not to do it. I'd hear a small voice warning me about things that were wrong or dangerous.

Now, some people might think that what's happening to me is a bad thing. But from the moment I left home this morning, not once have I been given any kind of sign opposing what I was about to do. Nothing.

What do you think this means? I'll tell you. People can never be harmed by doing what's right.

Usually we think death is bad. But maybe it's not. Death is one of two things. Either someone who's dead doesn't feel anything. Or it's like lucking out and getting a fancy new apartment. Instead of living in one place, you get to live someplace new.

If it's not feeling anything – like being asleep without dreaming – death would be a great gain. If someone had to choose between one night where he slept without dreams or worries of any kind, and all the other days and nights of his life, no man, not even a great king, could say for certain which he'd prefer. So if death is like this, it may be a gain. The whole of time would seem like one night.

On the other hand, if death is like being in a new place, and if it's true that those who've died are already there, then what could be better? If you arrived in Hades, having escaped those who pretend to be jurors, and found there the real jurors, those who judge justly – Minos and Aiacus and Triptolemus – would there be anything wrong with leaving home? Imagine Orpheus and Hesiod and Homer – all there together.

(*excitedly*)

How much wouldn't you give for that?

I'd want to die many times if this were true. I'd see and meet the most interesting and famous people. And I'd get to pester the biggest names that ever lived! I'd pass my time figuring out who was wise, and who thought he was wise, but wasn't.

Wouldn't it be great to be able to pester the men who led the army at Troy? Or Odysseus or Sisyphus? Or countless others one could mention, men and women alike? If I were there with them, talking and examining them, I'd be extraordinarily happy. It would be like one long philosophy seminar!

And they wouldn't be able to kill me for it either!

You can look forward to death, knowing this one thing: *bad things can't happen to good people.* Not when they're alive and not when they're dead.

*The* ARCHON, DIGNITARIES, *and* GUARD *finish their discussion. The* GUARD *approaches* SOCRATES.

SOCRATES (*cont'd*)

But I see it's time to go. Me to be put to death, and you to live. Only the gods know which of us is going to the better place.

# Act Three
## *Crito* and *Phaedo*

LEADER OF THE CHORUS

In Athens, executions were normally carried out immediately following a conviction. But in Socrates' case there was a delay of about a month. Every year the city sent a ship – the *Ship of Theseus* – to carry an offering to the island of Delos to honour the god Apollo. To maintain ritual purity, executions weren't permitted until the ship returned with news that the offering had been accepted.

While Socrates waited in prison, his lifelong friend Crito offered to help him escape. Socrates refused, even though this decision must have been hard for his wife, Xanthippe, to accept.

To fulfil the order of execution, Socrates had to drink a cup of hemlock, a type of poison. His last words, after the hemlock had begun to do its work, were that he and his friends owed a debt to Asclepius, the god of medicine.

Some commentators have understood these words to mean that Socrates' last concern, as he was preparing to enter the afterlife, was with the health of his soul. A much more likely explanation is that the offering was simply part of an annual religious festival that recognized the debt all Athenians owed to Asclepius for having recently delivered them from the plague.

Having just told all of Athens that he respected the gods of the city and that he was not a corruptor of the young, Socrates would have been especially concerned to observe the appropriate rituals.

As we return to the stage, we find Socrates asleep in his jail cell.
Dawn has just broken. Standing nearby, having bribed the guard to
let him in, is Crito.

SOCRATES' JAIL CELL, near the centre of Athens. Early morning. SOCRATES
lies sleeping on a crude bed. Standing nearby, looking out a small window is
CRITO. Through the window, CRITO sees that dawn has just broken. A rooster
crows. SOCRATES stirs.

SOCRATES

Crito, is that you?

CRITO

(without turning)
Yes.

SOCRATES

It's early.

CRITO

It is.

SOCRATES

How early?

CRITO

Just past dawn.

SOCRATES

I'm surprised the guard let you in.

CRITO

(still staring out the window)
We've become quite good friends. I told you he'd be willing to
bend a few rules, for a friend.

SOCRATES

Have you just arrived?

CRITO

I've been here awhile.

SOCRATES
Why didn't you wake me?

CRITO
I didn't want to disturb you.

SOCRATES
You didn't come to watch me sleep.

CRITO
(*turning, with some urgency*)
Time's running out. We have to discuss our plans. If we don't act soon, there won't be any time left.

SOCRATES
We've spoken of this before.

CRITO
But staying here to face an unjust execution – it's not right, letting your enemies have their way.

SOCRATES
There are worse things in life.

CRITO
Not many.

SOCRATES
You know it's never right to return a wrong for a wrong.

CRITO
(*impatiently*)
That's not the point! This whole mess has left your friends feeling ashamed! You know the charges should never have come to trial. It's time we made plans to have you sent away. The guards are willing to be bribed. And I have friends in Thessaly who'll take care of you.

SOCRATES
You know better than that.

CRITO

If you don't let us do what's right, people will think you died because we were cowards. Or that we didn't care. It doesn't have to be like this.

SOCRATES

Since childhood, I couldn't have asked for a better friend. But I need your clear head now more than ever. Let me ask you: would life be worth living with a body so completely diseased that it failed to serve any of its functions?

CRITO

(impatiently)
No, of course not.

SOCRATES

And what's more important, a healthy body or a healthy character?

CRITO

Stop it! I need you to focus on what's important.

SOCRATES

That's what I'm doing! Would life be worth living if that part of you – your heart, your soul, your character, whatever you want to call it – was so corrupt it no longer knew right from wrong?

CRITO is silent.

SOCRATES (cont'd)

Every wrong act damages a person's character. This one would do more damage than most.

CRITO

Stop it! That's not the situation we're in.

SOCRATES

That's exactly the situation we're in.

CRITO

(*angrily*)
The time for debate is over! For the sake of your family and your friends, it's time to do what's right!
(*regaining his composure*)
I just can't understand why you think this is the right thing to do. Especially when escape will be so easy.

SOCRATES

(*with mock seriousness*)
Do you know somewhere outside Athens where death can't reach me?

CRITO

Make fun of your friends if you like, but we only care about what's best for you.

SOCRATES

(*becoming serious*)
Then tell me, when someone's freely come to an agreement, should he break it? Or fulfil it?

CRITO

(*grudgingly*)
Obviously, he should fulfil it.

SOCRATES

And if I were to leave here now, wouldn't I be breaking a lifelong agreement?

CRITO

I don't see how.

SOCRATES

Imagine that as I was escaping, the city's laws came and confronted me.

*Two figures appear representing the laws, as if in a vision. They are strikingly reminiscent of the* STRONGER *and* WEAKER ARGUMENTS *in Aristophanes' play, although both now appear ready to argue about more serious topics.*

SOCRATES (*cont'd*)
They'd demand to know why I was escaping.

STRONGER ARGUMENT
We would.

WEAKER ARGUMENT
We'd need to know what evidence you had that this was the right thing to do. What argument can you give us that escape would be right?

SOCRATES
(*to* CRITO)
What should I say? Should I say that the city wronged me? That the jury's decision wasn't right for me or my children?

CRITO
Yes! By all the gods, that's exactly what you should say!

SOCRATES
Then I know what the laws will say:

WEAKER ARGUMENT
We'd ask, 'Was that our agreement? Did we agree that you would welcome our rulings only when you find them convenient? Was it that you should accept us only when you happen to think we're right?'

STRONGER ARGUMENT
Or was it that, by freely agreeing to live here, you'd help craft the best laws possible, and then abide by our decisions?

CRITO
If they came to you in this ridiculous fashion, you should ask them when you entered into such an agreement.

SOCRATES
I know what they'd say:

STRONGER ARGUMENT

You entered into this agreement every time you chose to live here and accept our protection, instead of moving somewhere else.

WEAKER ARGUMENT

You expressed your contentment with us every time you chose not to speak against us in the Assembly.

STRONGER ARGUMENT

And you acknowledged us every time you accepted the benefits we've given you, in peacetime and in war.

CRITO *considers responding, but says nothing.*

SOCRATES

Over the years we've all benefited from the protection of the laws. They've not only cared for us, but for our friends and families as well.

CRITO

But accepting a benefit isn't the same as entering into an agreement.

SOCRATES

That's true. But every time I've chosen to stay here, rather than go somewhere else, every time I've willingly relied on these laws, I've chosen them over others.

CRITO

Think of your sons!

SOCRATES

If I break the law now, what will I be saying to them? That I care more for my freedom than my word? At my trial I could have proposed banishment, and done with the laws' consent the very thing you now want me to do illegally.

STRONGER ARGUMENT

It's true.

CRITO *is thoughtful.*

WEAKER ARGUMENT

In a democracy you're only asked to do two things: obey the law, and try to change it if you think it's wrong.

STRONGER ARGUMENT

No city can survive if its laws are abandoned at the whim of every dissatisfied citizen.

SOCRATES

And by breaking the law, I'd harm myself even more than I'd harm the city. Doing wrong is never good for a person's character. Besides, if I show people that I think it's right to break the law, I'll have become exactly what I said I wasn't: a corrupter of the young.

CRITO *is silent.*

SOCRATES' JAIL CELL *near the centre of Athens. The next day.* SOCRATES *and* XANTHIPPE *are sitting together on the floor of the cell.*

XANTHIPPE

*(conspiratorially)*
Has Crito spoken to you?

SOCRATES

Almost every day.

XANTHIPPE

You know what I mean.

SOCRATES

About his plans?

XANTHIPPE

Yes.

SOCRATES

Yes.

XANTHIPPE

(*impatiently*)
And?

SOCRATES

It's too much to ask a friend to break the law.

XANTHIPPE

You're not asking. He's offering.

SOCRATES

That's true.

XANTHIPPE

Besides, it's a small price to pay to be able to raise our boys as you
know they should be raised.

SOCRATES

What kind of father would I be if I broke the law?

XANTHIPPE

Let Crito do what he wants.

SOCRATES

What would we tell the boys? It's not something we could hide
from them, you know.

XANTHIPPE

Any father's better than no father.

SOCRATES

You know that's not true.

XANTHIPPE

You know it's not that simple! Parents have to see that their children are properly brought up. Or they shouldn't have them in the
first place. Life isn't about making perfect decisions. It's about
doing the best you can in difficult circumstances.

SOCRATES

What do you want me to do? Run away some night when there's no moon? Hiding under an old goatskin cloak, as if I were a criminal? Take the boys to Thessaly where they'd live as fugitives?

XANTHIPPE

If you ask them, you know what they'd say.

SOCRATES

They're too young to know better. You know what I have to do.

XANTHIPPE

You know they deserve a father!

SOCRATES

You'll take care of them. And I'll ask Crito to take care of you.

XANTHIPPE

His offer is to take care of us all! He can easily afford to bribe the guards. He'll send us anywhere we want to go.

SOCRATES

You make it sound like he won't look after you if I'm dead. You know that's not true.

XANTHIPPE

There's more to being cared for than knowing where your next meal's coming from!

SOCRATES

That's exactly my point! What would you rather tell the boys? That I was killed by mistake, having done no wrong? Or that, because I was so greedy for life, I abandoned every value I've taught them to respect?

XANTHIPPE

Who cares what we tell them? As long as you're alive!

SOCRATES

You care a lot about what you tell them. Tell me now what you're going to say.

XANTHIPPE *is silent.*

SOCRATES (*cont'd*)
I thought so. Whether I die tomorrow, or two years from tomorrow, what does it matter? We've all had a death sentence pronounced on us since the day we were born.

XANTHIPPE
(*standing, angrily*)
I'll tell them their father was too pig-headed to know the difference between life and death!

CRITO *and several* FRIENDS *enter the cell.*

SOCRATES
You know what matters – the *only* thing that matters – is how we choose to live our lives before we die.

XANTHIPPE
(*angrily to* CRITO, *as she begins to leave*)
You talk to him! He's as stubborn as a mule, and twice as stupid!

CRITO
(*to* SOCRATES, *as* XANTHIPPE *leaves*)
I see you've been comforting your wife.

SOCRATES
Now don't you start!

SOCRATES' JAIL CELL *near the centre of Athens. The next day.* SOCRATES *and* XANTHIPPE *are in Socrates' jail cell, having spent the night together.*

XANTHIPPE
You've always been stubborn. Do you remember when Crito came for dinner? He's so rich. I was ashamed we had so little.

SOCRATES
The ship's returned from Delos.

XANTHIPPE
You said, 'Either he's a man of character, and he won't mind – '

SOCRATES

(*interrupting*)
The offering was accepted –

XANTHIPPE

(*interrupting*)
'Or he's not, in which case it won't matter.'

SOCRATES

Sometimes my tongue gets away from me.

XANTHIPPE

Oh, really?

As XANTHIPPE *kisses* SOCRATES *on his forehead,* CRITO *and several* FRIENDS
*(both men and women) enter the cell.*

SOCRATES

Here they are. I suppose they've come to say goodbye.

XANTHIPPE

Apollodorus said he wasn't going to come. He said he couldn't
bear to see you being put to death unjustly.

SOCRATES

(*jokingly*)
Would he prefer to see me being put to death *justly*?

XANTHIPPE

(*to* CRITO, *too sad to laugh at the joke*)
Is it time?

CRITO

It is.
(*as* XANTHIPPE *and the other* WOMEN *hug* SOCRATES *goodbye*)
The ship's returned. The offering's been accepted. The ban on executions has been lifted. Everyone wants to know how you are. I've
told them –

SOCRATES

(*interrupting*)
Will you see that the women get home safely?

CRITO

Of course.

CRITO *nods to one of the men accompanying him. The* MAN *exits with* XANTHIPPE *and the other* WOMEN *weeping.*

CRITO

The executioner stopped me on the way in. He says I'm to tell you to stay calm. When people get excited, the hemlock isn't as effective as it should be. People sometimes have to drink it more than once.

SOCRATES

Don't pay any attention to him.
    (*raising his voice so the offstage* EXECUTIONER *can hear him*)
Tell him he'd better be ready to give it to me two or three times. How else is he going to earn his pay?
    (*cheerfully, to the still offstage* EXECUTIONER)
Do you hear me?

CRITO

    (*to his* FRIENDS)
I figured as much.

*The* EXECUTIONER *enters, carrying a cup. He and* SOCRATES *appear to be on familiar terms.*

EXECUTIONER

What am I going to do with you?

SOCRATES

You're here early. It's to be a busy day, is it?

EXECUTIONER

You know this isn't something I'm looking forward to. Most people swear at me, and I have to fight with them to take the poison. But you. I'm only doing my job. They should be angry with the people who put them here. Not with me. But you.

SOCRATES

It's true, you don't have an easy job.

EXECUTIONER

Today will be hard –

SOCRATES

(*interrupting*)
Don't worry. I'll do what you tell me. As some character in a tragedy might say, my time's drawing near. Is everything ready?

CRITO

There's no rush. The rule is that it has to be done by sunset. But
many people wait until long into the night.

SOCRATES

I suppose it's natural to want to linger. But waiting will only make
me look foolish in my own eyes. My time's come.
    (*to the* EXECUTIONER)
You're the expert. What do I do?

EXECUTIONER

(*passing the cup to* SOCRATES)
Just drink it. Then walk until your legs feel heavy. Then lie down.
The rest will take care of itself.

SOCRATES

Can I pour a libation to the gods? We have a lot to be thankful for.

EXECUTIONER

I only mixed what I thought would be enough.

SOCRATES

Then we'll have to make do with a toast: May all our journeys be
fortunate ones!

SOCRATES *drinks the hemlock calmly and easily. His* FRIENDS *weep and cover
their faces.*

SOCRATES (*cont'd*)
Look at all this blubbering. This is why I sent the women away.

SOCRATES *walks around the room.*

SOCRATES (*cont'd*)
There's one other thing I need of you, my friends. When my sons grow up, measure their value. If they seem to be interested in anything more than virtue – anything at all – nag them about it, just as I've nagged you. If they have a reputation for pretending to be something they're not, call them on it. If you do this for me, both my sons and I will have been treated justly.
(*after a pause*)
I'm tiring.

EXECUTIONER
Then it's time.

SOCRATES *lies down on his bed.*

EXECUTIONER (*cont'd*)
Soon you'll begin to feel a numbness.

*The* EXECUTIONER *pinches his feet.*

EXECUTIONER (*cont'd*)
Can you feel this?

SOCRATES
No.

*The* EXECUTIONER *presses on his stomach.*

EXECUTIONER
And here?

SOCRATES
No.

EXECUTIONER
Then it's almost time. In a moment it will reach your heart.

SOCRATES
Then it's time to say goodbye.

*After his* FRIENDS *reach out to touch him and say goodbye,* SOCRATES *pulls the bed sheet above his head. He becomes still. Thinking he has died, his* FRIENDS *begin weeping. Unexpectedly* SOCRATES *lowers the sheet from his head.*

SOCRATES (cont'd)

Crito, we owe a rooster to Asclepius. Pay the debt, and don't forget.

CRITO

(*smiling*)
I won't. Is there anything else?

SOCRATES *gives no reply, having fallen silent for the last time. His eyes are fixed and his mouth is open.*

EXECUTIONER

He's gone.

*The* EXECUTIONER *closes* SOCRATES' *mouth and eyes and covers his face.* CRITO *uses his arm to wipe a tear from his eye.*

CRITO

Then it's time to say goodbye, and let history record these words:
Of all the men I've known, he was by far the wisest, most virtuous, and best.

*With these words, the sun sets and Athens falls into darkness. After a short pause, the lights go up. The stage is empty except for (one or more members of) the* CHORUS.

LEADER OF THE CHORUS

Among us there are those who weep,
Frightened still of death's long sleep.
Others look towards the clouds,
Alone, in fear of death's dark shroud.

We ask amid these tearful cries,
Were we right to call him wise?

He drank the hemlock, raised his arm,
Knowing no good man can come to harm.

There's so much more to life than tears,
More good than bad, in our few years.
If this is what we've learned today
We've done our part in this short play.

Goodnight!

*THE END*

# Notes

## Introduction

1 For a helpful explanation of the practices and conventions surrounding ancient Greek dates, see Nails 2002, xli–xliii.

2 For helpful synopses of all extant Greek plays from the fifth, fourth, and third centuries BCE, see McLeish and Griffiths 2003.

3 In the notes that follow, ancient sources such as those by Plato, Xenophon, Aristotle, and others are cited by a series of numbers (often combined with letters) common to all scholarly editions of these works. These numbers allow readers to check a citation without having to consult the same edition or translation used by the author. In the case of Plato and Plutarch, the numbers are called 'Stephanus numbers,' after the first modern editions of these works edited by Henricus Stephanus. In the case of Aristotle, the numbers are called 'Bekker numbers,' after the first complete works of Aristotle edited by August Immanuel Bekker.

4 Or at least that nothing he wrote survives. Cf. Plato *Phaedo* 60d; Diogenes Laertius *Lives of Eminent Philosophers* 2.18.

5 Diogenes Laertius *Lives of Eminent Philosophers* 2.48.

6 Xenophon *Socrates' Defence* 1. Some commentators warn that Diogenes Laertius can be unreliable on other matters as well, partly because he was separated from the people and events he was writing about by several hundred years and partly because of his uncritical reporting style. Since little is known of the circumstances of his life, it is also difficult to judge the reliability of his sources.

7 Other inconsistencies appear to be present in Plato's writings themselves. Among the most discussed are Socrates' views about democracy, death, and the moral authority of the law. For example, in the *Crito*, Socrates

argues strongly in favour of democracy (*Crito* 50a–54e), even though in the *Republic* he seems to argue for the opposite view (*Republic* 473c–e and passim). Similarly, in the *Apology*, Socrates seems to be non-committal about the possibility of life after death (*Apology* 40c–41c), but in the *Phaedo* he argues clearly in favour of a particular position (*Phaedo* 66e–69e). Finally, in the *Apology*, Socrates tells us there are circumstances in which he would be willing to disobey a democratically enacted law (*Apology* 38a), but in the *Crito* he seems to defend the view that disobeying such laws is never right (*Crito* 51a–52d). One explanation for such divergent reports could be that Socrates changed his mind about these issues over time. A more likely explanation is that Plato is sometimes reporting the views of the historical Socrates, but also sometimes using Socrates as a character in his dialogues to give voice to Plato's own (often quite different) ideas.

8  But see Colaiaco 2001, 17–21.
9  Plutarch *Moralia* 347c.
10 Herodotus *Histories* 6.105–106.
11 For an accessible introduction, see Garland 1990.
12 For a comprehensive but readable biography of this remarkable leader, see Kagan 1991.
13 Herodotus *Histories* 3.80.
14 Thucydides *History of the Peloponnesian War* 2.37.
15 Diogenes Laertius *Lives of Eminent Philosophers* 2.18.
16 Plato *Theaetetus* 151b.
17 For a helpful discussion about Greek education in general and about Socrates' influence on Athenian education in particular, see Beck 1964, esp. 188–98. Beck also relates the story of how Socrates' teacher, Prodikos, offered both a one-drachma course and a fifty-drachma course. Socrates' family was sufficiently prosperous to enrol him in the one-drachma course but not the fifty-drachma course (179–80). Cf. Plato *Cratylus* 384b.
18 Plato *Phaedo* 96a–e.
19 The people of the ancient city of Miletus lived within what is now modern-day Turkey. Like the Athenians, they oversaw a large maritime empire. Their influence was felt from Turkey to the Crimea.
20 Cicero *Tusculan Disputations* 5.4.10.
21 The two ideas are represented in Greek by the same word, *eudaimonia*.
22 The two ideas are again represented in Greek by a single word, *arete*.
23 Cf. Vlastos, 'Happiness and Virtue in Socrates' Moral Theory,' in Vlastos 1991, 200–32.
24 For an accessible introduction to the war, see Kagan 2003.
25 Plato *Symposium* 220d–e.

26  Ibid. 221a–c.
27  For a helpful compilation of the extant literature on this subject, see Hubbard 2003, esp. 163–267.
28  Plato *Charmides* 155d; Plato *Lysis* 203 ff.; Plato *Protagoras* 309a–d; Plato *Symposium* 213d and 216d; Xenophon *Symposium* [*The Banquet* or *The Dinner Party*] 4.27–28.
29  Cicero *De Fato* 5.10; Cicero *Tusculan Disputations* 4.37.80; Plato *Phaedrus* 238e ff.; Plato *Symposium* 217b–d, 219b–e; Plato (attributed) *Alcibiades* 103a; Xenophon *Memorabilia* [*Memoirs* or *Recollections*] 1.2.29–31, 1.3.8–14, and 2.6.28–33. Cf. Dover 1978, 153–70.
30  Pseudo-Lucian 'Forms of Love' 23.
31  Aristophanes *Clouds* 362; Plato *Symposium* 174a.
32  Diogenes Laertius *Lives of Eminent Philosophers* 2.122. Cf. Camp 1986, 145–7, for related discussion.
33  Plato *Apology* 30e.
34  Plato *Theaetetus* 152a.
35  Even so, in Plato's *Protagoras*, Protagoras sometime appears to be able to get the better of Socrates in argument. Socrates and Protagoras also appear to be on quite good terms.
36  Plato *Symposium* 215a–c, 221d–e; Plato *Theaetetus* 143e; Xenophon *Symposium* 4.19, 5.5–7. Cf. Richter 1965, 1:109–19; 1984, 198–204.
37  Diogenes Laertius *Lives of Eminent Philosophers* 2.26–7, 2.36–7; Xenophon *Symposium* 2.8–10.
38  Xenophon *Memorabilia* 2.2; Xenophon *Symposium* 2.10.
39  Attributed variously to Aeschines ('Socratics Letter 21'), Xenophon ('Epistle 8'), and others. For discussion, see Costa 2001 and Rosenmeyer 2006.
40  Aristotle *Fragments* F 93.
41  Plato *Phaedo* 60a; Plato *Halcyon* 8.
42  Diogenes Laertius *Lives of Eminent Philosophers* 2.26. Cf. MacDowell 1978, 90.
43  Diogenes Laertius *Lives of Eminent Philosophers* 2.26; Plato *Apology* 34d, 41e; Plato *Crito* 45c, 48c, 54a; Plato *Phaedo* 116b.
44  Xenophon *Memorabilia* 1.4.
45  For a helpful history, see Swaddling 1980.
46  Plutarch *Moralia* 414b.
47  Herodotus *Histories* 1.46–91.
48  Contemporary scholars have speculated that this likely would have occurred when Socrates was in his thirties, a few years prior to the premiere of Aristophanes' *Clouds*. Cf. Guthrie 1971, 85–6, and Reeve 1989, 21.
49  Plato *Apology* 21a. Cf. Xenophon *Socrates' Defence* 14–18. It is interesting to

note that although Plato reports the god as saying that no one was 'wiser' than Socrates, Xenophon reports the god as saying that no one was 'freer' than Socrates, 'or more just, or more moderate.' It is only by identifying wisdom with virtue (as Socrates did) that we are able to reconcile the two passages.

50  Xenophon *Memorabilia* 1.2.

51  Plato *Euthyphro* esp. 10a.

52  Cf. Aristophanes' *Clouds* 247–8, 364–7, 420–4, and passim, in which Socrates is portrayed as showing complete disrespect for the gods.

53  Plato *Apology* 38a.

54  Ibid. 41d.

55  Plato *Theaetetus* 150b–51d.

56  Aristotle *Politics* 2, 1265a12.

57  Plato *Apology* 24b. Cf. Plato *Euthyphro* 3b.

58  Xenophon *Socrates' Defence* 10. Cf. Xenophon *Memorabilia* 1.1.1, 1.2.9–61.

59  Diogenes Laertius *Lives of Eminent Philosophers* 2.40.

60  Plato *Apology* 26b; Plato *Euthyphro* 3c–d. Cf. McPherran 1996, chap. 3 ('Socrates and His Accusers').

61  Thucydides *History of the Peloponnesian War* 6.27–9, 6.53, 6.60–1; Xenophon *Hellenica* [*A History of My Times*] 1.4.13–21. See Nails 2002, 17–20, for a helpful overview.

62  Plato *Apology* 24e.

63  Ibid. 36a.

64  Ibid.

65  Diogenes Laertius *Lives of Eminent Philosophers* 2.41. According to Diogenes, 'He was condemned by 281 votes more than those given for acquittal,' which may be read to say that the difference between the number of votes cast for acquittal and the number of votes cast for conviction was 281, or that a total of 281 votes were cast for conviction and this was more than the number of votes cast for acquittal. If the former, and if Plato is right to suggest that the vote was a relatively close one, then the jury would have to have been much larger than 500 or 501. If the latter, and if Plato is right to say that the decision would have been reversed if only thirty of those who voted for conviction had voted instead for acquittal, then the jury would have to have consisted of 502 (or perhaps 503) members. Most likely, either there has been a transcription error over the centuries or else Plato's reference to thirty votes should be understood to mean *approximately* thirty votes.

66  Aristotle (attributed) *Athenaion Politeia* [*Constitution of Athens*] 39. Cf. Nails 2002, 219–22, for a helpful overview. See, too, Socrates' discussion in the *Apology* of his 'old accusers' (Plato *Apology* 18a–e).

67 For example, see Plato *Crito* 50a–54e, esp. 51b–c, 52a, and Diogenes Laertius *Lives of Eminent Philosophers* 2.24. Cf. Vlastos, 'The Historical Socrates and Athenian Democracy,' in Vlastos 1994, 87–108.

68 Xenophon *Memorabilia* 1.2.31–7.

69 Ibid. 1.2.11–28. Cf. Aeschines *Against Timarchus* 173; Aristophanes *Birds* 1281–3.

70 A helpful introduction appears in Camp 1986, 105, 107–113. See Colaiaco 2001, 13–14 (esp. n1) for additional references.

71 A helpful summary appears in the *Constitution of Athens*, although it needs to be remembered that Aristotle and his students were writing a generation after Socrates' trial. See Aristotle (attributed) *Athenaion Politeia* 57. Cf. MacDowell 1978, 24–40; MacDowell 1963, 33–89; and Stockton 1990, 96–103.

72 Plato *Euthyphro* 2a.

73 Cf. Xenophon *Socrates' Defence* 22.

74 Aristotle (attributed) *Athenaion Politeia* 57.

75 Plato *Apology* 36b.

76 For a helpful overview, see MacDowell 1978, 235–59.

77 Plato *Apology* 32a–c. Cf. Diogenes Laertius *Lives of Eminent Philosophers* 2.5.24; Xenophon *Hellenica* 1.7; and Xenophon *Memorabilia* 1.1.18, 4.4.2.

78 Plato *Apology* 32c–e. Cf. Diodorus Siculus *Bibliotheca Historica* [*Library of History*] 14.5.1–3.

79 Plato *Apology* 32e.

80 It is interesting to note that Socrates appears not to have held any lasting animosity towards Aristophanes, despite Aristophanes' unflattering portrayal of him in the *Clouds*. If Plato's writings are to be trusted, Socrates and Aristophanes socialized together and appear to have enjoyed debating with one another, at least on occasion (Plato *Symposium* passim).

81 Plato *Apology* 36d.

82 Ibid. 38b.

83 Diogenes Laertius *Lives of Eminent Philosophers* 2.41–2. Diogenes reports amounts of both 25 and 100 drachmas.

84 Plato *Apology* 36b–38b. Cf. Xenophon *Oeconomicus* [*The Estate Manager*] 2.3.4–5; Diogenes Laertius *Lives of Eminent Philosophers* 2.41–2, 2.121. For helpful biographical sketches of not only Crito, but also many of Socrates' other friends and acquaintances as well, see Nails 2002.

85 One drachma was roughly equivalent to a day's wage for a skilled labourer. Half a drachma was the fee paid for a day's jury duty.

86 Plato *Apology* 40a–c.

87 Ibid. 40c. Cf. Xenophon *Socrates' Defence* 2–10, 32; Plato *Theaetetus* 172.

88  Plato *Crito* 44c ff. Cf. Camp 1986, 113–16, for a helpful description of the prison itself.
89  Plato *Crito* 50a–54e.
90  For helpful discussion, see McPherran 2003.
91  Plato *Phaedo* 118a.
92  Diogenes Laertius *Lives of Eminent Philosophers* 2.43.
93  For a helpful overview, see Brickhouse and Smith 2000.
94  Aristotle *Rhetoric* 3.14.11, 1.9.30.
95  Aelian *Varia Historia* [*Historical Miscellany*] 2.11.
96  Xenophon *Socrates' Defence* 23.
97  Diogenes Laertius *Lives of Eminent Philosophers* 2.34.
98  Xenophon *Socrates' Defence* 28.
99  Diogenes Laertius *Lives of Eminent Philosophers* 2.35.
100  Plato *Crito* 53d.
101  Several additional anecdotes concerning Xanthippe appear in Aelian *Varia Historia* 7.10, 9.7, 9.29, 11.12.
102  Aeschines *Against Timarchus* 173; Xenophon *Memorablia* 1.2.
103  Plato *Phaedo* 116c.
104  Ibid. 118a.
105  Xenophon *Socrates' Defence* 34.
106  For example, the view is in direct contrast to Aristotle's comment in the *Nicomachean Ethics* that 'perhaps it is not the same in every case to be a good man and a good citizen' (1130b29).

## Production Notes

1  Plato *Laws* 876b. Cf. Plato *Apology* 21a; Xenophon *Socrates' Defence* 15.
2  Voting in Athenian trials appears to have taken the following form: upon entering the jury area, each juror was given two clay (or later, bronze) disks. Each disk had an axle through its centre — one hollow, the other solid. When the time came to vote, if jurors wanted to vote in favour of acquittal they deposited their disks with the solid axles in a bronze container. If they wanted to vote in favour of conviction they deposited their disks with the hollow axles. (The second disk was deposited in a wooden discard box.) By covering the ends of their axles with their thumbs and forefingers, jurors were able to keep their votes secret. Once the voting was complete, the disks from within the bronze container were hung on a pegboard for all to see. By placing the disks with hollow axles beside the disks with solid axles until there was a surplus of one kind or the other, even citizens who were unable to count could see whether the defendant was acquitted or convicted.

3 During at least one point in Athenian history, voters appear to have selected between proposed penalties by drawing a line on a wax tablet. A shorter line was used to vote in favour of the lesser of the two penalties; a longer line was used to vote in favour of the harsher of the two penalties.

4 Aelian *Varia Historia* [*Historical Miscellany*] 2.13.

## Classroom Notes

1 To learn more about how ancient Greek plays were originally performed, students may wish to consult Wiles 2000, and McLeish and Griffiths 2003.

2 To learn more about everyday life in ancient Greece, students may wish to consult Flacelière 2002, especially chap. 6 ('Dress and Toilet'); Garland 1990; and Massey 1988.

3 To learn more about the workings of Athenian courts, students may wish to consult MacDowell 1978.

## Pronunciation of Greek Names

1 For a detailed history of the development of the Greek language across the centuries, see Horrocks, 1997.

2 For guidance on the pronunciation of ancient Greek words as they would have been pronounced in Socrates' day, see Allen 1974.

# Bibliography

## Ancient Sources

Aelian. *Historical Miscellany*. Translated by Nigel G. Wilson. Loeb Classical Library. Cambridge, MA: Harvard University Press, 1997.

Aeschines. *Aeschines*. Translated by Christopher Carey. Austin: University of Texas Press, 2000.

Aristophanes. *The Acharnians, the Clouds, Lysistrata*. Translated by Alan H. Sommerstein. London: Penguin, 1973.

– *Aristophanes 1: Clouds, Wasps, Birds*. Translated by Peter Meineck. Indianapolis: Hackett, 1998.

– *Clouds*. Translated by K.J. Dover. Oxford: Clarendon, 1968.

– *Clouds, Wasps, Peace*. Translated by Jeffrey Henderson. Loeb Classical Library. Cambridge, MA: Harvard University Press, 1998.

Aristophanes, Plato, and Xenophon. *The Trials of Socrates: Six Classic Texts* [*The Clouds, the Euthyphro, the Apology, the Crito, the Phaedo, Socrates' Defense to the Jury*]. Edited by C.D.C. Reeve. Indianapolis: Hackett, 2002.

Aristotle. *The Complete Works of Aristotle*. Edited by Jonathan Barnes. Princeton: Princeton University Press, 1995.

Cicero [Marcus Tullius]. *Tusculan Disputations*. Translated by J.E. King. Loeb Classical Library. Cambridge: Harvard University Press, 1950.

Diodorus Siculus. *Library of History*. Translated by C.H. Oldfather. Loeb Classical Library. Cambridge: Harvard University Press, 1933.

Diogenes Laertius. *Lives of Eminent Philosophers*. 2 vols. Translated by R.D. Hick. Loeb Classical Library. London: Heinmann, 1925.

Diogenes Laertius, Libanius, Maximus of Tyre, and Apuleius. *The Unknown Socrates* [*The Life of Socrates, Apology of Socrates, Whether Socrates Did the Right Thing When He Did Not Defend Himself, On the God of Socrates*]. Edited by William M. Calder III. Translated by Bernhard Huss, Marc Mastrangelo, R. Scott Smith, and Stephen M. Trzaskoma. Wauconda, IL: Bolchazy Carducci, 2002.

Herodotus. *The Histories*. Translated by Aubrey de Sélincourt. Harmondsworth: Penguin, 1972.

– *The Persian Wars*. 4 vols. Translated by A.D. Godley. Loeb Classical Library. Cambridge: Harvard University Press, 1920.

Plato. *Complete Works*. Edited by John M. Cooper and D.S. Hutchinson. Indianapolis: Hackett, 1997.

– *Defence of Socrates, Euthyphro, Crito*. Translated by David Gallop. New York: Oxford University Press, 1999.

– *Euthyphro, Apology, Crito, Phaedo, Phaedrus*. Translated by H.N. Fowler. Loeb Classical Library. Cambridge, MA: Harvard University Press, 1914.

– *The Last Days of Socrates* [*The Euthyphro, the Apology, the Crito, the Phaedo*]. Translated by Hugh Tredennick and Harold Tarrant. Harmondsworth: Penguin, 1959.

– *Phaedo*. Translated by David Gallop. Oxford: Clarendon, 1975.

– *The Trial and Death of Socrates* [*The Euthyphro, the Apology, the Crito, the Phaedo*]. Translated by G.M.A. Grube. Indianapolis: Hackett, 1975.

Plutarch. *Lives of the Noble Greeks*. Edited by Edmund Fuller. New York: Dell, 1959.

– *Moralia*. 16 vols. Translated by Frank C. Babbitt et al. Loeb Classical Library. Cambridge, MA: Harvard University Press, 1927–2004.

– *Parallel Lives*. 11 vols. Translated by Bernadotte Perrin. Loeb Classical Library. London: Heinemann, 1914–26.

Pseudo-Lucian. 'Forms of Love.' In Thomas K. Hubbard, *Homosexuality in Greece and Rome: A Sourcebook of Basic Documents*, 505–53. Berkeley: University of California Press, 2003.

Thucydides, *History of the Peloponnesian War*. Translated by Rex Warner. Harmondsworth: Penguin, 1972.

Xenophon. *Conversations of Socrates* [*Socrates' Defence, Memoirs of Socrates, the Dinner Party, the Estate Manager*]. Translated by Hugh Tredennick and Robin Waterfield. London: Penguin, 1990.

– *A History of My Times*. Translated by Rex Warner. Harmondsworth: Penguin, 1979.

– *Memorabilia*. Translated by Amy L. Bonnette. Ithaca: Cornell University Press, 1994.

– *Memorabilia, Oeconomicus, Symposium, Apology*. Translated by O.J. Todd. Loeb Classical Library. Cambridge, MA: Harvard University Press, 1923.

– *The Whole Works of Xenophon*. Translated by Ashley Cooper et al. London: Jones, 1832.

## Modern Sources

Ahbel-Rappe, Sara, and Rachana Kamtekar. *A Companion to Socrates*. Oxford: Blackwell, 2005.

Allen, W. Sidney. *Vox Graeca: A Guide to the Pronunciation of Classical Greek*. 2nd ed. Cambridge: Cambridge University Press, 1974.

Annas, Julia, *Plato: A Very Short Introduction*. New York: Oxford University Press, 2003.

Arnott, Peter D. *An Introduction to the Greek Theatre*. Foreword by H.D.F. Kitto. London: Macmillan, 1959.

Barnes, Jonathan. *Aristotle: A Very Short Introduction*. New York: Oxford University Press, 2001.

Beck, Frederick A.G. *Greek Education 450–350 BC*. London: Methuen, 1964.

Benson, Hugh H. *Essays on the Philosophy of Socrates*. New York: Oxford University Press, 1992.

Bonner, Robert J. *Lawyers and Litigants in Ancient Athens*. Chicago: University of Chicago Press, 1927.

Brickhouse, Thomas C., and Nicholas D. Smith. *The Philosophy of Socrates*. Boulder: Westview, 2000.

– *Plato's Socrates*. New York: Oxford University Press, 1994.

– *Socrates on Trial*. Princeton: Princeton University Press, 1989.

– *The Trial and Execution of Socrates: Sources and Controversies*. New York: Oxford University Press, 2002.

Brunschwig, Jacques, and Geoffrey E.R. Lloyd. *A Guide to Greek Thought: Major Figures and Trends*. Cambridge, MA: Belknap, 2003.

Burkert, W. *Greek Religion*. Cambridge, MA: Harvard University Press, 1985.

Burnyeat, Myles F. 'The Impiety of Socrates.' *Ancient Philosophy* 17 (1998): 1–12.

Camp, John M. *The Archaeology of Athens*. New Haven: Yale University Press, 2001.

– *The Athenian Agora: Excavations in the Heart of Classical Athens*. London: Thames and Hudson, 1986.

– *The Athenian Agora: A Guide to the Excavation and Museum*. 4th ed. Athens: American School of Classical Studies at Athens, 1990.

Camp, John M., and Elizabeth A. Fisher. *The World of the Ancient Greeks*. New York: Thames and Hudson, 2002.

Colaiaco, James A. *Socrates against Athens: Philosophy on Trial*. New York: Routledge, 2001.

Cooper, J.G. *The Life of Socrates*. London: Dodsley, 1749.

Cornford, Francis M. *Before and after Socrates*. Cambridge: Cambridge University Press, 1932.

Costa, C.D.N. *Greek Fictional Letters*. Oxford: Oxford University Press, 2001.

Dover, K.J. *Greek Homosexuality*. Cambridge, MA: Harvard University Press, 1978.

Ferguson, John. *Socrates: A Source Book*. London: Macmillan, 1970.

Flacelière, Robert. *Daily Life in Greece at the Time of Pericles*. Translated by Peter Green. London: Phoenix, 2002.

Garland, Robert. *The Greek Way of Life*. Ithaca, NY: Cornell University Press, 1990.

Grote, G. *Plato and Other Companions of Socrates*. 3 vols. London: Murray, 1865.

Guthrie, W.K.C. *Socrates*. Cambridge: Cambridge University Press, 1971.

Horrocks, Geoffrey. *Greek: A History of the Language and Its Speakers*. New York: Longman, 1997.

Hubbard, Thomas K. *Homosexuality in Greece and Rome: A Sourcebook of Basic Documents*. Berkeley: University of California Press, 2003.

Jones, A.H.M. *Athenian Democracy*. Baltimore: Johns Hopkins University Press, 1986.

Judson, Lindsay, and Vassilis Karasmanis. *Remembering Socrates: Philosophical Essays*. New York: Oxford University Press, 2006.

Kagan, Donald. *The Peloponnesian War*. New York: Viking, 2003.

– *Pericles of Athens and the Birth of Democracy*. New York: Free Press, 1991.

Kraut, Richard. *Socrates and the State*. Princeton: Princeton University Press, 1984.

Lang, Mabel L. *Socrates in the Agora*. Princeton: American School of Classical Studies at Athens, 1978.

Levin, Richard L., and John Bremer. *The Question of Socrates*. New York: Harcourt Brace and World, 1961.

Livingstone, R.W. *Portrait of Socrates*. Oxford: Clarendon, 1938.

MacDowell, Douglas M. *Athenian Homicide Law*. Manchester: Manchester University Press, 1963.

– *The Law in Classical Athens*. Ithaca: Cornell University Press, 1978.

McLeish, Kenneth, and Trevor R. Griffiths. *A Guide to Greek Theatre and Drama*. London: Methuen, 2003.

McPherran, Mark L. *The Religion of Socrates*. University Park: Pennsylvania State University Press, 1996.

– 'Socrates, Crito, and Their Debt to Asclepius.' *Ancient Philosophy* 23 (2003): 71–92.

Massey, Michael. *Women in Ancient Greece and Rome*. Cambridge: Cambridge University Press, 1988.

Millett, Paul. 'The Trial of Socrates Revisited.' *European Review of History* 12 (2005): 23–62.

Nails, Debra. *The People of Plato: A Prosopography of Plato and Other Socratics*. Indianapolis: Hackett, 2002.

Ober, Josiah. *Political Dissent in Democratic Athens*. Princeton: Princeton University Press, 1998.

Parker, Meg. *Socrates and Athens*. Bristol: Bristol Classical, 1973.

Phillipson, Coleman. *The Trial of Socrates*. London: Stevens, 1928.

Reeve, C.D.C. *Socrates in the* Apology. Indianapolis: Hackett, 1989.

Richter, Gisela M.A. *The Portraits of the Greeks*. 3 vols. London: Phaidon, 1965. Abridged and revised in a single volume by R.R.R. Smith. Oxford: Phaidon, 1984.

Roberts, J.W. *City of Sokrates: An Introduction to Classical Athens*. 2nd ed. London: Routledge, 1998.

Rosenmeyer, Patricia A. *Ancient Greek Literary Letters*. New York: Routledge, 2006.

Ross, W. David. 'The Socratic Problem.' *Proceedings of the Classical Association* 30 (1933): 7–24.

Smith, Nicholas D., and Paul Woodruff. *Reason and Religion in Socratic Philosophy*. New York: Oxford University Press, 2000.

Stockton, David. *The Classical Athenian Democracy*. New York: Oxford University Press, 1990.

Stone, I.F. *The Trial of Socrates*. London: Cape, 1988.

Strauss, Leo. *Socrates and Aristophanes*. Chicago: University of Chicago Press, 1966.

Swaddling, Judith. *The Ancient Olympic Games*. London: British Museum, 1980.

Taylor, A.E. *Socrates*, London: Davies, 1932.

Taylor, Christopher. *Socrates: A Very Short Introduction*. New York: Oxford University Press, 2000.

Vander Waerdt, Paul. *The Socratic Movement*. Ithaca: Cornell University Press, 1994.

Vlastos, Gregory. *Socrates: Ironist and Moral Philosopher*. New York: Cambridge University Press, 1991.

– *Socratic Studies*. New York: Cambridge University Press, 1994.

Wiles, David. *Greek Theatre Performance: An Introduction*. Cambridge: Cambridge University Press, 2000.

Winspear, A.D., and T. Silverberg. *Who Was Socrates?* New York: Cordon, 1939.

Zeller, E. *Socrates and the Socratic Schools*. Translated by O.J. Reichel. London: Longmans, Green, 1868.

## Other Modern Plays about Socrates

Alastos, Doros. *Socrates Tried*. London: Zeno, 1966.

Anderson, Maxwell. *Barefoot in Athens*. New York: Sloane, 1951.

Bax, Clifford. *Socrates: A Play in Six Scenes*. London: Gollancz, 1930.

Bregstein, Barbara. 'Socrates on Trial.' Wings Theatre / Educational Theater of New York, New York, 2004.

Frey, Barbara. 'Clouds.' Athens New Theatre / Hellenic American Union, Athens, 1973.

Hibbert, Paul, and Oliver Segal. 'The Clouds.' Wadham College / Oxford University Classical Drama Society, Oxford, 1984.

Laird, Fiona. 'The Clouds.' Shaw Theatre / London Small Theatre Company, London, 1990.

Love, Harry. 'The Clouds, or The Lowest Form of Higher Education.' University of Otago / Classics Department, Dunedin, 2001.

Radzinsky, Edvard. 'Conversations with Socrates.' Translated by Alma Law. Jean Cocteau Repertory, New York, 1986.

Richards, I.A. *Why So, Socrates? A Dramatic Version of Plato's Dialogues Euthyphro, Apology, Crito, Phaedo.* Cambridge: Cambridge University Press, 1964.

Robic, Greg. 'Clouds.' Poor Alex Theatre / Ancient Comic Opera Company, Toronto, 1995–6.

Sinclair, Lister. *Socrates: A Drama in Three Acts.* Illustrated by Kay Ambrose. Notes by G.L. Keyes. Agincourt, ON: Book Society of Canada, 1957.

Swash, Colin. 'The Man Who Argued Himself to Death.' Michaelhouse Theatre, Cambridge, 2005.

Target Margin Theater. 'Dinner Party.' The Kitchen / Target Margin Theater, New York, 2007.

Tomlinson, Edward. 'The Clouds.' The Courtyard / Kaloi k'Agathoi, Hereford, 2007.

Topol, Josef. 'Goodbye Socrates.' Stavovské Theatre, Prague, 1976.

Voltaire. *Socrates: A Tragedy of Three Acts.* Translated by Mr Fatema. London: Dodsley, 1760.